MIDDLE DISTA[NCE]

Contemporary Theory, Technique and Training

Third Edition

EDITED BY JESS JARVER

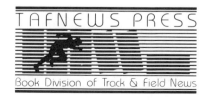

TAFNEWS PRESS

Book Division of Track & Field News

First published in 1991 by Tafnews Press,
Book Division of Track & Field News
2570 El Camino Real, Suite 606
Mountain View, CA 94040 USA.

First edition printed in 1979
Second edition printed in 1985
Third edition, with all-new material, printed in 1991

Standard Book Number 0-911521-34-8
Printed in the United States of America

Cover design by Teresa Tam
Production: Grace Light, Teresa Tam

PHOTO CREDITS

Cover	Suzy Favor (1990 NCAA)	ALLSPORT/Ken Andersen
Title page	Sydney Maree (1981 NCAA)	Bill Killian
13	Steve Scott	Doug Wells/*Des Moines Register*
24	Sebastian Coe	Nick Brawn
39	Christine Wachtel, et al.	Horstmüller
50	Joaquim Cruz	Horstmüller
64	Jarmila Kratochvilová	Rhein-Ruhr-Foto/Gustav Schröder
65	PattiSue Plumer, et al.	Jeff Johnson
77	Marcello Fiasconaro	
85	Simon Doyle	Horstmüller
95	John Trautmann	Jeff Johnson
117	1984 Women's NCAA 1500	Jeff Johnson

ACKNOWLEDGEMENTS

The publishers wish to thank the following publications for their cooperation and permission to reprint articles that originally appeared in their pages:

A COLLECTION OF EUROPEAN SPORTS SCIENCE TRANSLATIONS, Jess Jarver, Editor. Published by S.A. Sports Institute, P.O. Box 219, Brooklyn Park, S.A. 5032, Australia.

ATHLETICS COACH, Julie Dennis, Editor. Published by the British Amateur Athletic Board, Edgbaston House, 3 Dutchess Place, Hagley Road, Birmingham B16 8NM, England.

DER LEICHTATHLET, Peter Gran, Editor. Published by Deutscher Verband fur Leichtathletik der DDR, Dimitroffstrasse 157, Berlin 1055, German Democratic Republic.

DIE LEHRE DER LEICHTATHLETIK, published as part of *Leichtathletik.* Helmar Hommel, Editor.

FI/ETS MAGGLINGEN, Dr. Hanspeter Probst, Editor. Published by Eidgenossiche Turn-und Sportschule, Magglingen CH-2532, Switzerland.

JUOKSJA, Ari Paunonen, Editor. Helsinki, Finland.

KEHAKULTUUR, Roland Hurt, Editor. Published by Perioodika, Tallinn 200 102, Suur-Karja II, Estonia, USSR.

KESK-JA PIKAMAA JOOKS, by Alfred Pisuke and Ants Nurmekivi. Published by Eesti Raamat, Tallinn 200 090, Parnu Mut. 10, Estonia, USSR.

LEICHTATHLETIK, Heinz Vogel, Editor. Published by Deutscher Sportverlag Kurt Stroof GMBH, Eintrachtstrasse 110-118, 5000 Koln 1, Germany .

LEISTUNGSSPORT, Peter Tschiene, Editor. Published by Deutscher Sportbund, Otto-Fleck-Schneise 12, 6000 Frankfurt 71, Germany.

LEGKAYA ATLETIKA, 103021 Moscow K-31, Rodjeatvensk Bulvar 10/7, USSR.

MODERN ATHLETE AND COACH, Jess Jarver, Editor. Published by Australian Track and Field Coaches Association, 1 Fox Avenue, Athelstone, S.A. 5076, Australia.

SPORTLIK TREENING, by Dr. Atko Viru. Published by Eesti Raamat, Tallinn 200 090, Parnu Mut. 10, Estonia, USSR.

TECHNICAL BULLETIN, Roman Olszewski, Editor. Published by Ontario Track and Field Association, 1220 Sheppard Avenue E., Willowdale, Ontario M2K 2X1, Canada.

TRACK & FIELD QUARTERLY REVIEW, George G. Dales, Editor. Published by the NCAA Division I Track & Field Coaches Association, 1705 Evanston, Kalamazoo, Michigan 49008. USA.

TRACK TECHNIQUE, Jed Goldfried, Editor. Published by Track & Field News, 2570 El Camino Real, Suite 606, Mountain View, California 94040, USA.

TABLE OF CONTENTS

CHAPTER III: APPROACHES TO TRAINING

CHAPTER IV: THE YOUNG MIDDLE DISTANCE RUNNER

translation is by Dr. Kuulo Kutsar.

INTRODUCTION

CONTEMPORARY DEVELOPMENTS IN MIDDLE DISTANCE RUNNING

by Jess Jarver

Training for middle distance events is a complex process in which a series of interrelated performance factors are developed and improved. Dominating among these factors are the athlete's aerobic and anaerobic work capacities to exploit efficiently the available energy sources for a particular distance. As experience has shown, the development of the two major performance capacities, combined with such allied factors as speed, strength and muscular endurance, is by no means an easy task.

On the contrary, as the selection of articles in this text will show, there are several problems to be solved in the planning, execution and monitoring of middle distance training. To start with there is the task of finding the correct training load, dependent not only on the volume, but also on the type and structure. The next problem, after the determination of the load, is its distribution to achieve optimal development, as well as to reach peak form at the right time.

The most complicated task, considered by many experts to be the most critical, is to determine training intensity. This applies particularly to the development of aerobic endurance, a subject that has lately been frequently discussed in sport science literature. Since biochemistry started to dominate training control the determination of training intensity has become closely related to the still debated concept of the anaerobic threshold.

As if this is not enough, we are still faced with the choice of training means and methods to most effectively improve the vital performance factor. The choice applies not only to the best approach to develop the required performance factors but also must be adapted to the athlete's individual characteristics. Identical training procedures simply are not always responsible for success in different athletes.

Add to it the development of speed, speed endurance, muscular strength and muscular endurance factors and it becomes obvious that the planning and guidance of training in middle distance running is a rather complicated task. Consequently, the views presented in this text vary on several aspects of endurance development. Such differences occur not only among practicing coaches, but also among physiologists, as far as controlling the training intensities is concerned.

There is no doubt that performances in middle distance running have improved considerably thanks to the contributions from sport scientists. Biochemistry has played an important role here since analysis of blood lactate accumulation during intensive physical work was introduced as a training control. The introduction of biochemistry to middle distance training led to the concept of "anaerobic threshold," which has become the key parameter, as well as controversial subject, in endurance training.

The anaerobic threshold is defined as the point where the lactate accumulation signifies the change from aerobic to anaerobic energy supply. Sometimes referred to as the lactate threshold, it depends not only on the intensity of the exercise but also on its duration. In testing procedures the anaerobic threshold is determined as being the point where a deviation occurs in the lactate graph. Otherwise an arbitrary fixed value of lactate, equal to 4 mmol/l, is accepted as the anaerobic threshold.

While the determination of the anaerobic threshold is considered extremely important to find the most efficient training intensities, the concept is not irrefutable and can lead to training under "false" intensities due to testing errors. This controversial and often debated situation is well summed up in the article "The Anaerobic Threshold—From Euphoria to Confidence Crisis" by Manuel Bueno of Switzerland.

Bueno claims that "the threshold concept is not a dogma and consequently we must accept its results, not as an obligation, but rather as a direction . . . If interpreted under medical guidance, the threshold can provide a practical parameter for the planning of training, particularly when it is accompanied by field tests."

An accepted and reasonably reliable field test is the Conconi Test, named after Professor Conconi of Italy. It is based on the fact that the heart rate increases linearly until the work load leads to greater energy needs and a change to use of anaerobic energy sources takes place. Although the Conconi Test has been criticized by several sport scientists, it nevertheless has been universally accepted as a guide to endurance training. The details of the Conconi Test are presented in Hanspeter Probst's article in great detail.

Looking at other factors involved in the organization of middle distance training reveals that sport scientists list aerobic power, anaerobic capacity, anaerobic power and running economy as the most important parameters contributing to the performance. As William Black of the USA points out in his article "The Scientific Bases of Training for Middle Distance Running," knowing the qualities makes it possible to:

• Choose the proper training means and methods
• Organize them into an effective system of training.

Unfortunately, as the reader will find out, no clear-cut answer to how the optimal training means and methods will be found and organized is available. There appears to be lack of a common approach, which is no wonder when individual characteristics of an athlete have to be taken into consideration. It is therefore interesting to note that several authors recommend the use of what they call complex methods.

Phil Lundin of the USA, for example, recommends the mixing of various endurance development means throughout the yearly training cycle, stressing different ones at different times. Ants Nurmekivi of Estonia believes that the dominant methodology at the present time is to combine methods and techniques in which the ratio of different loads is adjusted according to the specific demands of the event and the athlete's individual characteristics.

Nurmekivi draws attention to the statement of the Soviet scientist Bedkovsky, who claims "that the training of middle distance runners should be both complex and individualized complex." In other words, the method must be adapted to the athlete, not the athletes, with their strengths and weaknesses, to the method.

Views also differ slightly when it comes to the organization of the training means and methods into an effective training year. It appears that simple single and double periodized years are still common, although the original concept of Matveyev, who divided the year into transition, general preparation, specific preparation and competition periods, has lost its appeal.

Adam Zajac and Gregory Prus of Poland, for example, recommend in their article on middle distance training that the traditional concept of annual training cycles has to be changed in order to meet today's competition demands. They present a new, more elastic, structure that allows for high level performances throughout the year by including three major training phases—accumulation, intensification and transformation—regularly in most micro and mesocycles.

Ray Lapinski of Australia comes to similar conclusions in his article "Variations in Middle Distance Running Training." Lapinski's complex method, in direct contrast to Lydiard's system of periodization, is based on many types of training throughout weekly or bi-weekly cycles. However, he emphasizes that a strong aerobic background is required before this method is employed.

Obviously such changes in periodization also require extreme care in the planning of micro and mesocycles to provide for a proper balance between volume and intensity, as well as work and recovery. The new regimen must secure regeneration before the start of each new microcycle, a factor particularly important during competition mesocycles.

The importance of restoration is strongly stressed by Dr. Atko Viru of Estonia in his discussion of the contemporary trends in the construction of microcycles. He suggests that each microcycle must be concluded with one or two recovery days, although it is not uncommon to divide a microcycle so that the recovery takes place between two loading phases.

While on the subject of restoration, it is interesting to note that most experts agree that overtraining occurs most often from the intensity of a forced training load. Intensity, therefore, appears to play a key role in the organization of middle distance training, most likely a vital role when multi-session training days are employed.

Contrary to the different views and opinions

concerning periodization, virtually all authors are in agreement in the chapter dealing with the training and development of young middle distance runners. Ari Paunonen of Finland, introducing the views of Olav Karikosk, sums it up perfectly in stressing the need to avoid early specialization. He criticizes the questionable values of the training systems developed by many well known coaches and asks: "Are we going to repeat the regretful mistakes of the past by stressing anaerobic training at an early age?"

As can be seen from this short introduction, sport science's contribution has been responsible for a number of changes in contemporary middle distance running training. Research has identified the major physiological factors that contribute to performance and has provided guidelines for the controlling and monitoring of training.

However, the available knowledge is still short of information regarding the best biochemistry-guided training control and the most effective system of training. Consequently, conflicting views will appear in this text, as no attempt has been made to provide uniformity. It is therefore wise to keep in mind that the organization of training in middle distance running must be adapted to individual characteristics of an athlete. Runners with different physiological makeup will reach their potential by using varying approaches to training.

CHAPTER I

GENERAL PRINCIPLES

SOME FACTS ABOUT THE CONSTRUCTION OF MICROCYCLES IN TRAINING

by Dr. Atko Viru, Estonia, USSR

The author discusses the construction and the tasks of different types of microcycles in training, delving in detail into accumulating and varied loads microcycles.

MICROCYCLES

Microcycles in training are responsible for the coordination of training loads to establish an effective balance between work and recovery. This regimen must provide sufficient regeneration before the start of each new microcycle. This means that the function of a microcycle is to provide a rational approach to the exploitation of the training loads planned for a particular training phase.

The duration of a microcycle is usually one week, although athletes who are training twice or even three times a day often plan slightly shorter microcycles. As a rule, each microcycle is concluded with one or two recovery days. Most common among the variations are 6+1, 5+2, 4+1 and 3+1, in which the first number indicates consecutive training days, the second the number of recovery days.

A microcycle consists of two phases—the development stimulating phase and the restorative phase. The first applies to the use of training loads, the second to recovery loads or complete rest (Matveyev 1977). The restoration phase usually takes place at the end of a microcycle. However, it is not uncommon to divide a microcycle so that the recovery takes place between two load phases.

There are several possibilities to classify microcycles according to the training processes. Based on Matveyev's classification microcycles are divided into four main categories: 1. developmental, 2. preparation, 3. competition and 4. restorative microcycles.

The developmental microcycle, according to the nature of the employed training methods, is adjusted to general preparation or to specific preparation. In both cases the microcycles are subdivided into ordinary and shock cycles. In the ordinary development microcycles the training load and intensity are increased gradually. In the shock cycles the load undergoes an extreme lift by the increase of the volume or the intensity. The shock microcycles aim for general conditioning in the first part of the preparation period, and event specific development in the second part.

The preparation microcycles ensure the readiness of an athlete for the forthcoming competitions. At the same time, the last preparation microcycle before a competition has to mobilize the athlete's performance capacities. For some athletes this could require training with reasonable workloads. For others it means tapering by using a reduced load or active rest with restoration processes.

The competition microcycles are designed to organize activities just prior to and immediately after a competition. This involves activities a day before the competition, on the day of the competition, and during the recovery days. The organization of the competition microcycles is individual and depends on the length of the competition, the number of attempts, the frequency of competitions, the performance level of the rivals and so on.

The main task of the restorative microcycles is to create the best possible conditions for recovery. This means training with moderate intensity and a reduced volume, combined with all available regeneration measures.

ACCUMULATING LOADS

A further classification of microcycles can be based on the different coordination of training loads.

The two common methods used in this classification are the accumulating loads and the varied loads microcycles.

The effect of the accumulation of several consecutive loads show that the restoration of speed, anaerobic and aerobic work capacities remain unchanged (Fig. 1). However, it can be seen that two consecutive speed training sessions are responsible for a drop in speed and delayed restoration. A somewhat similar situation can be noted in the anaerobic work capacity, showing the problems created by similar consecutive loads.

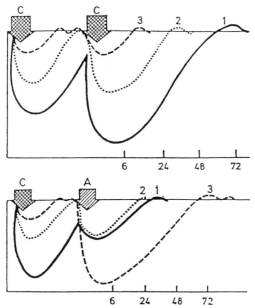

Figure 1: Recovery dynamics between two loads. Same direction (above), Different directions (below). C = speed training, A = endurance training, 1 = speed, 2 = anaerobic capacity, 3 = aerobic capacity.

There are no basic differences in the restoration dynamics when three consecutive loads are applied (Fig. 2), making it clear that the accumulation of several similar direction loads is responsible for fatigue and lengthens the restoration processes of corresponding work capacities.

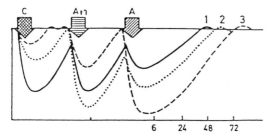

Figure 2: Recovery dynamics after three different direction loads. C = speed; An = anaerobic, A = speed, 2 = anaerobic capacity, 3 = aerobic capacity.

Studies of microcycles with a 4+1 combination of accumulating loads showed that it can lead to exhaustion in some athletes. In this situation it is up to the coach to change from the development stimulating phase to the restoration phase in time. For example, the studies by Baikov came to the conclusion that developmental loads can be continued until the specific work capacity has dropped by 30%. At this stage training has to be changed for 2 to 3 days of recovery loads, followed by another 2 to 3 days of maintenance loads. Rest days are introduced after 2 to 3 microcycles.

Platonov (1986) summed up the shortcomings of similar accumulating loads in microcycles as follows:

- The accumulating of fatigue is responsible for a drop in the general work capacity of an athlete
- There is a lack of balance in the development of the different performance capacities
- There is a possibility that over-training occurs.

VARIED LOADS

Varied loads microcycles aim to exploit the dynamics of recovery processes in order to employ the largest feasible total work volume for the training effect. There are two possibilities to achieve this aim:

1. By alternating maintenance and restoration loads for the effective use of several large loads within a microcycle.
2. By alternating the direction of the loads within a microcycle through switching the basic load on the already recovered function.

The duration of recoveries of the various metabolic parameters are presented as a guide in Table 1. As can be seen the restoration of some functions take a considerable time. It should be noted here that there is a difference in the restoration dynamics between different and similar consecutive loads. Figure 1 (bottom) gives an example where aerobic endurance training follows speed training.

There is no accumulating influence on the speed and anaerobic capacities but the aerobic work capacity drops after the second training session. A similar situation occurs when three different consecutive loads are applied—speed development, followed by anaerobic and aerobic endurance development (Figure 2).

Obviously, the largest drop and the slowest recovery of the work capacity takes place in the indicators involved in the previous training session. There appears to be no accumulation of fatigue in other indicators (Platonov, Vaitsehhovski, 1985). this confirms the theory that the use of different loads allows the use of recovery time for other training tasks. Skillful changing of loads therefore allows the athlete to begin each following workout in good condition to tackle opposite direction training loads.

It is generally recommended that a microcycle is designed so that large loads in speed and power development take place udner optimal conditions. To speed up the recovery processes after heavy loads the following training session should include medium or light loads that are definitely aimed in another direction. It is advantageous to develop speed, flexibility and strength in small muscle groups daily, while the development of large muscle groups should take place every second day. It is important to keep in mind that the varied load microcycles aim not only to purposefully exploit the recovery phase but also to speed up recovery.

Table1: Efficient sequences of training loads in one day (Platanov, Verhoshanski, 1985)

Metabolic Parameter	Minimal Time	Maximal Time
Muscle ATP and creatin-phosphate	2 min.	5 min.
Muscle glycogen reserves	5 hrs.	48 hrs.
Liver glycogen reserves	not known	48 hrs.
Excessive blood lactate	30 min.	2 hrs.
Muscle oxygen reserves	10-15 min.	1 min.
Intensive synthesis of enzymes and structural carbohydrates	12 hrs.	72 hrs.

Table 2: Minimal and maximal restoration times of different metabolic parameters

Basic Training (Heavy Load)	Supplementary Training (Medium or Light Load)
1. Development of basic speed capacities, improvement of speed technique	Development of aerobic capacity, steady method
2. Development of anaerobic work capacity for event specific endurance	Development of aerobic capacity, steady method
3. Development of aerobic work capacity for event specific endurance	Speed training, improvement of speed technique
4. Complex training in order of speed, aerobic and anaerobic work capacities	Complex training or the development of aerobic capacity, steady method Speed training
5. Complex training—aerobic and anaerobic capacities in parallel	
6. Complex training—speed and anaerobic capacities in parallel	Development of aerobic capacity, steady method

MULTIPLE TRAINING SESSIONS

Practical experience has shown that several training sessions are needed in a daily routine to reach top level performances. In track and field it is generally accepted that a microcycle for high performance athletes must include 6 to 8 basic and 7 to 12 supplementary training sessions (Ozolin, Homenkov, 1987). The number of training sessions in a microcycle are often increased during the preparation period and can in some cases be doubled.

In the beginning multiple daily training was approached by simply dividing a heavy training load between two sessions. This helped to reduce the drop in the work capacity in comparison to one heavily loaded workout. It also was discovered that the work capacity was restored faster when the load was divided into two workouts on the same day.

Nevertheless, contemporary knowledge indicates that there is no justification in the division of the same load into several training units. This will only make it difficult to increase the load and takes away the possibility of influencing the recovery by medium loads of a different nature. Training two or three times a day will not only allow an increase in the load, but also allows the work to be distributed more efficiently (Ozolin, Homenkov, 1982).

A multi-session training day is, as a rule, made up of one basic workout, supplemented by one or two additional sessions (morning, evening). The morning sessions are usually light and have a limited load on the organism. The basic workout must achieve the planned tasks for a particular day, while the evening sessions are usually of a restorative character. The use of two basic workouts a day can be justified only when athletes of a very high performance level have to stimulate the organism in a limited time period.

There is a danger that several training sessions a day can lead to fatigue and overtraining. To avoid this requires close cooperation between the coach and the doctor, as well as access to biochemical testing. At the same time, it is essential to keep in mind two main reasons for extreme fatigue:

1. The lack of a rational sequence in the order of different training loads
2. Failure to consider the influence of the previous load on the athlete's organism in the planning of the next load.

Finally, the importance of recovery and restoration must be stressed in the structure of microcycles. The total load of a microcycle can be increased considerably by the speeding up of restoration processes. At the same time it is important not to overlook the influence on the restoration processes on the training effect. It is not always positive. Without going into the details of the complex problems of restoration, it can be said that the methods usually are made up of the following:

- Organizational (the right combination of training loads and the correct time intervals between the training units)

- Psychological (favorable influences in the transfer from work to recovery and later in the transfer from recovery to work)
- Physiotherapeutic (including, among others, massage and sauna)
- Pharmacological (only under medical control).

TACTICS IN MIDDLE DISTANCE RUNNING

by Paul Schmidt, Germany

A simple and practical guide on how to plan successful racing tactics in middle distance running with a checklist of the most important tactical rules.

The realization of a competitive performance that corresponds to the actual performance potential of a middle distance runner is decisively determined by the planned race tactics, as well as psychological and physiological factors. The tactical organization of a race can therefore be defined as "a goal to arrange the race under existing conditions so that the achieved result corresponds to, or even exceeds, the actual performance capacity."

The planning of successful competition tactics requires the evaluation prior to the race of the following important components:

- What is the estimated level of the athlete's own performance capacity? This question can be answered with the help of the results and race analysis of recent competitions, taking into consideration race conditions. The toleration of specific training loads and the results of time trials also assist.
- What is the estimated performance level of the rivals? What are their recent results?
- Have several athletes from one club or one nation dominated the race?
- Is there a pacemaker in the race?
- When is the race held?
- Are there heats? What is needed to qualify for the final?
- What is the correct length of spikes?
- What are the weather conditions to be taken into consideration?
- Where is the warm-up area situated? What is the reporting time?
- How and when should travel to the competition venue take place?
- When should the last meal before the race take place and what should it contain?
- Are split times to be called out? If yes, at what points in the stadium?

- Would calling out encouragement have a positive stimulating effect?

Only with these references is it possible to arrange the necessary race preparations without hectic last minute decisions. The cautious planning also has a calming effect on the athlete, promoting self-confidence. Experienced coaches therefore analyze the above information carefully and make preparations to implement the plan without burdening the athlete.

WARM-UP BEHAVIOR

An optimal physical and psychological performance preparedness depends on correct procedures in the warm-up area. It should be treated as the preliminary part of the race itself. The behavior in the warm-up area decides whether the total performance potential is activated, or if only part of it is mobilized due to serious shortcomings in the undertaken procedures.

It is easy to recognize successful middle distance runners during their warm-up. They are, assisted by the coach, able to switch off all disturbing factors and concentrate completely on their warm-up ritual. Their behavior is "tactically" correct before the actual race.

The following is characteristic of an experienced, highly motivated high performance athlete:

- He finds, if the venue allows it, a place or path away from his rivals to complete his race preparations. Strong winds, rain or high temperatures influence the choice of the warm-up procedures
- He warms up alone and is not influenced by the warm-up procedures of his rivals
- He rehearses mentally the race tactics planned

with the coach. The decisive actions are visually performed, but enough flexibility is allowed for deviations from the planned strategy in case the race proceedings require a change.

The coach restrains himself. It is sufficient for the athlete to know that the coach is available at any time to solve problems that occur during the warm-up. Eye contact and a few words of encouragement in the right situation means more than a flood of useless information.

CARDINAL ERRORS

- To leave the inside lane in order to pass in situations when this is not absolutely necessary. The difference between the inside lane and lane two is 7.04m. An 800m runner, who stays mainly in the second lane and runs at the same pace as his rival on the inside lane, will be a full second behind in a 1:50 race
- A defensive, hesitant race performance. Chances for a possible victory or a good placing are simply given away
- The loss of contact with the leader(s) without an evident reason, without even an effort to activate physical and psychological energy sources
- No control over yourself and over the race activities of the closest rivals
- Unnecessary, performance affecting, position changes
- Looking around for rivals. It upsets the running rhythm and economy, leading to poorer end results
- To reduce speed before the finish line. How often in the history of major championships and important races has this led to the loss of a medal or the elimination from the final. It is inexcusable behavior
- To depend too much on having split times called out
- To pull out of a race without a really urgent reason. Pulling out can be substantiated only for health reasons. In all other cases the psychological suffering from giving up will be more damaging than finishing the race below expectations.

IMPORTANT TACTICAL RULES

The most important tactical rules can be traced from the main cardinal errors. A middle distance runner, who avoids the cardinal errors, or who commits them only once, behaves tactically correctly and has an optimal race strategy. Nevertheless, this author believes that it is useful to outline the most important rules in the format of a checklist. An offense against these rules is virtually always responsible for a drop in performance and often also for a poorer placement in the race.

It is amazing how many athletes have difficulties in the application of these rules in the often spontaneously changing situations of middle distance races. Apparently the psychological demands of the competition make it difficult to apply the easy-to-learn principles and rules, making experienced athletes often look like raw beginners.

The checklist of the most important tactical rules reads as follows:

1. With the help of your coach set yourself a realistic performance target for each race. Next solve the race strategy problems by finding ways and means that provide the best possibilities to achieve the planned target.
2. Keep in mind that the track is exactly 400m long (30cm from this line during a middle distance race has all the shortcomings of allowing yourself the "luxury" to run further than the competition distance requires). Sound tactics are to remain in the inside lane during the race as long as possible and leave it only in an exceptional situation in order to get into a better position or to avoid being boxed in.
3. It is often valuable during the early parts of a season to attempt to win races from the leading position. Nobody, besides your coach, will know when you plan this tactical move in a race. It helps to develop your courage to take risks and improves your willpower.
4. If you are looking to improve your personal best, plan with your coach realistic split times for the distance, taking into consideration your actual performance capacity. Plan for an even pace and try to avoid sudden accelerations. However, be flexible and prepared to make changes when the race situations dictate deviations from your plan. Keep in mind that major championships have their own "rules" that differ considerably from the usual national and international meetings. It is therefore inadvisable to plan for certain split times in major championship races.
5. The starting position influences the initiative and the behavior after the starter's gun has been fired. If you happen to have drawn one of the inside lanes, attempt to reach the leading position in the field. This helps to prevent being boxed in or changing the running rhythm. It always is possible to give up the leading position by opening the inside lane after the first curve in

the 800m or after 40 to 60m, in the 1500m.

If you happen to draw an outside position try, after the start and before reaching the next curve, to find a position that doesn't upset your chances in the following proceedings in the race. Only clearly superior athletes can afford to stay at the end of the field in the early stages of the competition.

6. You should pass on the curve only when there is no other way to find a better position and even then by staying as close to the inside lane as possible. Otherwise all passing maneuvers should take place in the straights. You should constantly strive to stay as close as possible to the inside of the track because the aim is to cover the actual racing distance and not a single meter more.

7. In case of a strong headwind, stay with the leaders but avoid being the first runner in most cases. Being in front in these circumstances reduces the chances of winning or being well placed.

8. A maximal effort, without looking around, is a must in the home straight until you are at least two meters past the finish line. Use an active arm action, as this is a proven method to maintain speed under extremely fatigued conditions.

SPONTANEOUS ACTIONS

World class middle distance runners stand out with their spontaneous reflexes and tactical actions that take place as a reaction to the moves of their rivals, or when certain situations call for a fast, reflexive decision. This author is not sure if such tactical reaction capacities can be developed, because it appears that some specific genetic prerequisites play an important part. However, there is no doubt that attempts to try out several tactical variations help to develop spontaneous flexibility. This means that it is advisable to set tasks in training and in racing to widen the tactical possibilities.

The tactical shape of a race reflects the character of an athlete. It reveals the athlete's courage, determination, intuition and something that can be called distance specific intelligence. However, it also reveals at the same time lack of attention and overconfidence when the finger is raised to signify victory shortly after passing the rivals in the home straight.

Aim to win! If this, despite the mobilization of all resources, is not possible, try to achieve the best possible time and placing. By following this principle there is never any reason to be disappointed, even if you don't win.

Table 1: A sample race strategy for a target time around 1:46.0 in an 800m race with the aim of the best possible final placement.

1.	Start	— A fast start. The pace is adjusted to reach the second position in the field in the back straight. First 100m in 12.5 seconds.
2.	Back Straight (200m)	— Run undisturbed on the inside lane. To reach the 200m mark in 25.5 seconds.
3.	Second Curve	— Remain on the inside lane. Keep even pace and check your running technique.
4.	Home Straight (400m)	— Remain in second or third position. If the pace is too slow take the lead. Avoid being boxed in. Reach the 400m mark in 51.5 seconds.
5.	Third Curve	— Try to remain on the inside lane. Check running technique and relaxation.
6.	500m	— Reach the mark in 65.0 seconds.
7.	Back Straight (600m)	— Stay with the leaders, or even lead. Avoid getting boxed in and aim to reach the 600m mark in 78.0 seconds.
8.	Fourth Curve	— Try to remain on the inside lane without being boxed in.
9.	Home Straight	— You will make it! Use active arm action and don't look around. Exploit all your strength until you are 2m past the finish line.

THOUGHTS ABOUT ADAPTATION IN MIDDLE DISTANCE RUNNING TRAINING

by Ants Nurmekivi, Estonia

The dominant methodology in contemporary middle distance running is to employ complex training methods and means to be adapted to the athlete's individual characteristics and tolerance to training loads.

The specifics of middle distance running training can be viewed from two different angles. The first is from the standpoint of the competition distance, ranging from 800m to 2000m. The second is from the standpoint of the athlete's individual characteristics that determine the body's reaction to the different types of training loads.

ENERGY SOURCES

It is a well known fact that the longer the distance, the greater is the contribution from aerobic energy sources to the performance. However, an effective adaption to a particular racing distance also depends on genetics. The most important genetic contribution comes from a favorable distribution of muscle fiber for a particular competition distance. The ratio of the different types of muscle fibers decides the athlete's potential for achieving a high level of the essential enzymatic activity and a high level of maximum oxygen uptake (VO$_2$ max).

A certain ratio is required between fast-twitch (white) and slow-twitch (red) fibers in order to perform successfully. Although most authorities claim that the ratio of muscle fibers is genetically determined, some studies have shown that changes can occur in their biochemical characteristics. It appears possible that a portion of fast-twitch fibers approach the characteristics of slow-twitch fibers after prolonged high volume training.

Several studies have indicated that aerobic endurance depends not so much on the oxygen transport to the working muscles as on the ability of the muscles to utilize the available oxygen. The oxygen utilization processes, in turn, depend on:

- The density of the capillary network
- The hemoglobin level in the blood
- The quantity of mitochondria
- The activity of enzymes of the mitochondria.

Table 1: Energy sources in middle distance running.

Energy source (%)	Distance (m)		
	400	800 (1:54.0)	1500 (3:40.0)
Aerobic	18.5	35	52.5
Anerobic	81.5	65	47.5

The above-mentioned processes occur mainly in the red muscle fibers to create a high oxidative potential. At the same time, favorable conditions are created to utilize lactate formed in the white muscle fiber. This leads to more economical aerobic processes and helps to preserve the relatively limited reserves of glycogen and creatine for the later stages of the race. An effective finishing kick in middle distance running depends largely on the available quantity of glycogen and creatine phosphate.

Many studies associated with oxygen utilization in the muscles have involved hypoxia. These studies have shown that hypoxia doesn't increase with an increased power output. A load of 100% of VO$_2$ max is consequently responsible for the most effective stimulus for chemical changes in the muscles. If the load exceeds 100% of the VO$_2$ max, the stimulus doesn't increase.

Workloads, performed at critical speed over two to three minutes with two to three minute recoveries, are considered to be most effective in developing aerobic power. This procedure creates a complex effect on the muscle fibers, because the fast-twitch fibers are activated when the VO$_2$ max level reaches

22

90%. The recoveries prevent excessive lactate accumulation and consequently make it possible to increase the training effect to 30 minutes and even longer. Without recovery intervals the same workout would be limited to only 10 to 12 minutes.

The minute volume of the heart has a critical role in the transport of oxygen and is usually developed by employing extensive interval running. Excessive intense running that exceeds the body's adaptive capacity must be avoided. While it may lead to a rapid growth in the heart volume, it also can create a disproportion between the increased heart volume and its functions.

Studies also have shown that oxygen utilization at the local muscular level drops much faster than the central oxygen transport system when training is restricted or stopped. In addition, the development of local muscular endurance needs intensive training and requires more time than the development of the autonomous central system. Experience indicates here the value of specific strength training in the development of local muscular endurance, provided the methods employed do not increase muscle mass. The correct sequence of motor units is no less important.

The above-mentioned facts indicate that performances in distance running depend largely on the heart muscle that receives its energy from aerobic processes. Middle distance running simultaneously requires a high capacity of anaerobic processes.

ADAPTATION TO TRAINING

The general requirements in the planning and conducting of training are the same for all distances, namely:

- A progressively increased training load
- Variations in intensity
- The maintenance of all aspects of training throughout all periods, changing only the ratio of their volumes.

THE 800m

The main energy supply mechanism in the 800m is the anaerobic-glucolite system. Consequently, athletes who are genetically prepared for anaerobic work by having a relatively high percentage of fast-twitch muscle fibers are better suited for this distance.

Sebastian Coe, reported to have a 50:50 ratio of fast-twitch and slow-twitch fibers, is a typical example. His fiber distribution also shows why he was equally successful over the 1500m distance, an event depending on both aerobic and anaerobic energy sources. What is needed is a good top speed, as well as a high level of specific endurance.

In training it is best to place emphasis on the genetically determined stronger aspects in the selection of a suitable training load. It is even better when these aspects coincide with the specific demands of a particular event. If they don't, attempts should be made to compensate for the shortcomings. This, however, is most difficult as far as speed is concerned.

Experience has shown that the most effective way to increase the aerobic endurance capacity of a "fast" 800m runner is the use of long continuous runs at sub-anaerobic threshold speeds. Jumping exercises and uphill running are the best suited to develop local muscular endurance and athletes with a high level of glycolitic capacity are advised to make more use of shorter than competition distances in training.

THE 1500m

Although anaerobic and aerobic energy sources have a nearly equal role in the 1500m, different combinations can be observed in individual runners. For example, there are athletes who have a high anaerobic capacity (good over 800m) but only a moderate aerobic capacity (mediocre 5000m times). In this case excessively intense anaerobic training would be ineffective and could lead to rapid fatigue.

Emphasis during the specific preparation period should always be on the development of the stronger performance aspects of an athlete. Athletes who belong to the so-called "endurance" type should avoid intensive interval sessions and include them in the program only once a week. Athletes with better anaerobic capacities, on the other hand, are advised to avoid high volume interval running over longer distances. They would benefit more from emphasizing shorter repetitions.

It is vital to employ extensive interval running at the beginning of the specific preparation period. This is necessary to:

- Increase the oxidative capacity of the slow-twitch (red) muscle fibers
- Improve the athlete's capacity to utilize lactate
- Develop the intermedial muscle fibers (particularly in uphill running)
- Achieve the neuromuscular coordination close to the speed of the competition event
- Reduce the discrepancy between the oxidative and glycolitic fibers through a shift to a more economical aerobic energy supply.

This creates a solid foundation for the following intensive interval and repetition running to develop glycolitic capacities over the next month or two. Thus, the various aspects of training, emphasized in certain training phases, lead towards the expected results.

IN CONCLUSION

In conclusion it can be said that the dominant methodology in middle distance running training at the present time is to employ combined methods and techniques. The ratio between the different loads is adjusted according to the specific demands of the event, the athlete's individual characteristics and the athlete's tolerance to certain training loads.

It is appropriate here to draw attention to the statement made by Dedkovsky, who claimed that the training of middle distance runners should be both "complex" and "individualized complex." In other words, the method must be adapted to the athlete, not all the athletes with their strengths and weaknesses to the one method.

Sebastian Coe's reported 50:50 fast-twitch/slow-twitch fiber distribution helps explain his similar outstanding success at both 800m and 1500m.

BASIC PHYSIOLOGY IN MIDDLE DISTANCE RUNNING

by Graham R. Ward, Ph.D., Canada

A summary of the influences of the universally employed training methods in middle distance running on the physiological-biological development of athletes.

PHYSIOLOGICAL—BIOLOGICAL DEVELOPMENTS

1. Continuous Endurance Exercise

- Cardiovascular regulation, capillarization, oxygen uptake in blood, and changes in metabolism of muscle appear to strengthen will power or determination (physiological)
- Develops general endurance, local endurance of muscle and endurance for the specific event
- Develops "steady-state" functioning which is at equilibrium with oxygen, i.e., homeostasis of the body functions. Body uses its own reserves and eliminates oxygen debt. The key is to balance the systems
- Develops a large ability to consume oxygen maximally (VO_2 max) and thus most long distance exercisers develop large VO_2 max values. The larger the value the better the prospects are for good performances. However, a very large VO_2 max does not carry with it an assurance of success. In fact, in marathon running VO_2 max (ml/kg/min.) is really poorly correlated with running speed. The fastest marathoner could sustain about 86% of his VO_2 max for long periods, yet had a 69 ml/kg/min. which is lower than the top runners. Middle distance performers are usually lower
- A high oxygen transport system implies that a particular energy output can be achieved with less strain. This also carries over to anaerobic events where an excellently trained athlete with high aerobic power usually can do better specific training. It appears that the better the O_2 transport system is, the better the athlete recovers and is able to achieve more training work. The central circulation, the heart and the peripheral circulation are all trained by an aerobic program. The central circulation is improved when large muscle mass is worked, while the peripheral circulation is trained best if the specific muscles of the training (event) are employed. The oxygen uptake also in many cases increases considerably from 3-4 L/min. to over 6L/min. When the oxygen uptake is related to body weight some athletes have obtained values of 85 ml/kg/min. (cross country skiers) compared to anything from 35-45 ml/kg/min. for the normal population
- Heart rate is a good guide to aerobic work. According to many scientists when the heart rate is about 130 beats/min., oxygen uptake is near 50% of VO_2 max and at 150 beats the uptake climbs to 60% and at 170 beats the oxygen uptake approaches 78-80% VO_2 max. Also with long work the pulse rate drops by 30-40 beats/min. To do this, the beat should be 150/170/min.
- From aerobic work other changes occur—erythrocytes work more, the heart volume works and hemoglobin % climbs
- The cardiac output also works from normal for men of about 17-20 L/min. for non-active people or 23 L/min. for active ones to over 30 L/min. Stroke Volume also increases both at rest and at stress. It goes from 68± ml to about 194 + ml/beat and athletes can utilize about 95% of their max. stroke volume, but during long exercise the stroke volume usually drops about 10-13 ml/beat and at the same time the cardiac output rises about 10% after about 20 minutes of exercise. With aerobic exercise the gas exchange increases and the central nervous system also develops if the exercise load is kept constant throughout the training

over prolonged periods.

AEROBIC ENDURANCE FACTORS

1. **Training with Prolonged Exercise Periods and Lower Intensity**
   (Main Functional Effect = endurance and aerobic capacity).
2. **Develop Endurance**
   a. Exercise at least 3-4 minutes.
   b. Exercise large muscle groups.
   c. Systems associated with an oxidative supply (heart, lung, blood, enzymatic) are required to adapt.
3. **Training with Above Regime**
   a. Increases aerobic capacity.
   b. Measured by maximal oxygen intake.
   c. Related to the specificity of training, ability to work for prolonged time spans is best developed by exercising for long periods.
   d. Must exercise the whole body which works against fatigue.
   e. Training speed for long distances requires only approximately 60% of maximal capacity but the exercise period is 1-3 hours with total workload being very high.
   f. Aerobic training improves basic cellular oxidative capacity, since energy cost for prolonged work is mainly covered by oxidative processes.
   g. During resting, heart rate often reduced to 38-50 beats/minute.
   h. Heart develops economy—lowers pulse rate and increases beat volume leading to larger reserves for stressful exercise. During long exercise (1 hour +) with heart rate 160-170 beats/minute, only slight rise of lactate seen at beginning of exercise. End lactate similar to rest before exercise.
   i. Respiratory system also develops increased oxygen consumption—vital capacity of lung can increase from 3-4.5L to over 6L.
   j. Develop better equilibrium of metabolic processes—called "steady state" in distance training.
      • Respiration, blood pressure, pulse rate and motor units in nerve systems, etc., become stable
      • Oxygen, blood flow, energy use and by-products of contractions at equilibrium in muscle
   k. Oxygen debt in distance work is about 3-6% compared to 90-95% for sprinters.

---

2. **Interval Work**
   a. **Extensive**

   • **Tempo Runs**
     Executed by extensive intervals—develop basic endurance. This comes about from the volume, short interval "break" and the extended time the training takes. Development depends upon length and speed of exercise which could be between 60-80% of best performance

     Can also develop specific endurance which is determined by short exercise periods or medium exercise intensities

Oxygen-intake influences endurance level. Cardiovascular system improves circulation by gradually increasing load on large volumes of work

During the development period, young athletes are helped metabolically when interval exercising by an increased heart size and stroke rhythm. Later, after a few months of this work, there is a change in stroke rhythm. The heart size frequently decreases but the stroke volume increases considerably. This also occurs in young teenagers

• **Fatigue**
  How does fatigue get delayed?

  ❏ Nervous system (central) fatigue
  ❏ Muscular system (local peripheral) fatigue

"Central" always appears to precede the "peripheral" fatigue but they are very closely related. Because there is a high demand of oxygen which is usually in limited supply, the acids produced (lactate) inhibit the firing potential of the nerves because the acid cannot be split. After a number of repeats the muscle goes into oxygen debt and the acid impedes the nerve. Unfortunately, the nerve cell tires out first and the motor unit stops firing and in turn the muscle also stops contracting.

Extensive intervals are important to help to improve the capacity of the blood to bind more oxygen which eventually reaches the muscle cell and bathes it with more fuel.

This type of work also increases the muscle cross-section (hypertrophy) and the density and size of the capillaries, which in turn leads to less fatigue and a better and quicker recovery. The pulse rate also lowers at rest.

b. **Intensive**

• Develops speed-endurance, short and medium endurance, strength, speed and explosive force
• In this very demanding anaerobic work the muscle and the body overall are under

extreme stress, and are continually in oxygen debt

- After each bout of exercise, there is an excess oxygen intake in comparison to the resting value before exercise and it is the resting value which is used to calculate the amount of oxygen deficit. It would appear from the inadequate oxygen intake that the body may go into an oxygen debt of up to 20 liters, which is repaid after the exercise and partially before the next exercise effort

- This leads to the situation where the muscle has to work mainly under anaerobic conditions (without a good supply of usable oxygen). If the athlete took a longer "break" after the exercise, the oxygen debt would be paid back within about 5-6 minutes or less; of course, this would then defeat the "intensive interval" situation and the training by this method would be wasted

- During vigorous exercise like this the muscle is under considerable metabolic stress where the glycolytic rate increases 100 times ± and the blood system has to work harder to clear the build-up of the acid metabolites (lactate) and other products such as CO_2. The blood has to neutralize these products with its buffering ability. After intense exercise the lactate is removed when some of it is converted to CO_2 and eliminated via the respiration. The remaining lactate is taken up in the blood and transferred from the cells to other tissues such as the liver, resting muscle and the kidney to form glucose and glycogen

- Actually the lactate formed is highest a few minutes after the exercise is finished and can be explained in part by the fact that there is not an immediate inhibition of glycolysis, but still a high glycolytic breakdown and little oxidation of lactate and pyruvate. However, in highly trained athletes the lactate is lower than in poorly trained people working at the same load, and there is faster oxidation. In addition, because there is an increase in mitochondria during intensive work there is a doubled capacity for pyruvate oxidation causing the athlete to produce less lactate. If the intensive intervals are less than 200m there can be little lactate produced. With the intensity of exercise

(75%) there are changes also in the cross-section of muscle, making the fibers larger, the capillaries more dense, but only if the repetitions are sufficient (4-10). Because of better vasodilation a greater supply of oxygen can get to the cells and, in turn, a better energy supply is set up which helps forestall fatigue

- This type of work also builds up glycogen and glycolytic enzyme reserves far quicker than other forms of training appears to do

- Training by this method appears to promote nervous system adaptations because the resting (break) periods are too short for a full recovery. A better metabolic resistance also develops and faster body movements (speed) result.

c. **Repetition Work**

- Usually the exercise creates strong reactions in the central nervous system. This type of exercise (90-100% effort) must be very carefully controlled because nerve ending failure and other metabolic inhibitions may result because of the heavy muscle contractions involved. However, the 90-100% efforts are very valuable at the correct time of the competitive season because of the extreme stresses which in turn cause high blood and muscle lactate production and nerve system fatigue.

The adaptations from this exercise are the delaying of fatigue and other metabolic shifts. Changes occur in this type of work in a similar way to the intensive interval work, but this exercise is often more demanding

- Other training adaptations are the development of speed endurance, speed and maximum strength.

ENDURANCE

1. **Long Term** (Intensity, Volume, Duration)
   Be able to continually work for 11-12 minutes to several hours at a generally constant pace. The intensity is between 70-95% of the athlete's speed during racing. This is mainly, if not almost completely, under aerobic conditions.
   Quite often divided into subsections:

   a. 11-12 minutes ➡ ➡ ➡ 30 minutes (3km-10km)

b. 31 minutes ➡ ➡ ➡ 90 minutes (10km-25km)

c. 91 minutes and beyond (25km+)

- Beginning Juniors
- 5 minutes to 45 minutes of work at even medium pace. Do time runs at same pace out and back and do that for 5 months
- Judge development by speed of second half of the run. If speed changes, adjust distance: shorten or lengthen
- Judge development by pulse rate
- Load — low   140-160+
        — medium   160-175+
        — high   175-190+
- The medium range after 3 months is a good load for 30 minutes
- Distances ➡ ➡ ➡
    12 yrs (14 yrs) = 8km
    12-16 (18 yrs) = 3 ➡ ➡ ➡ 16km
    16 (18 yrs) to adult = 3 ➡ ➡ ➡ 25km

Continuous (Long) Term		
General Preparation		
	km	Minutes
Short Distances	2-8	8-36
Middle Distance	5-20	17-90
(i) Women	5-15	17-65
(ii) Men	10-20	38-90
Long Distance	25-30	100-150
Advanced Preparation		
	km	Minutes
Short Distance ➡➡	10	40-45
Middle Distance	10-20	35-85
(i) Women	10-18	35-85
(ii) Men	10-20	35-85
Long Distance	20 ➡➡	86-140
All work is with a continuous load.		

2. **Medium Term** (1000m ➡ ➡ 3000m+)

a. Be able to cover about 2-11 minutes. Usually both aerobic and anaerobic components are used.

b. Strength and speed endurance are important components as distance covered employs quite rapid movement.

3. **Short Term** (400m-900m+)

a. Be able to cover about 45 seconds to 120 seconds. Usually highest component is anaerobic metabolism. Short term level development depends on strength and speed endurance and is known as **Interval Work.**

4. **Speed Endurance** (sub-maximal to maximal)
This type of training is carried out to help arrest fatigue during anaerobic work. After training repeatedly for a few weeks at speed over short distances the result is that the athlete is less impaired by fatigue and other detrimental metabolic shifts.

5. **Strength Endurance**
The idea here is to develop strength combined with stamina. Best improved by mixing various stimuli. Training with various types of **Intervals** is a major way to build strength, speed and local muscle endurance because the exercise and rest periods are regularly altered.

The interval is the **Break** or less active resting period between the activity (repetitions). The break can be **Complete** (long rest) or it can be shorter and **Incomplete.**

INTERVAL EXERCISE

Depends Upon Load

a. **Extensive**
- Total exercise load is done with large volume in time

b. **Intensive**
- Total exercise load is done with large volume in time

Extensive Work

1. **Intensity**
- Usually lowish (medium) intensity and can also be with or without weights. As running intensity between 60-80% but as strength exercise usually 50-60% of maximum capacity.

2. **Volume**
- If low intensity, large volume. If medium intensity with "break", more repetitions are possible fatigue factors usually delayed.

3. **Density**
- Exercises usually done closer together. The break (jogging recovery) between exercise is usually fairly short. For advanced, trained athletes the break is between 45 seconds to 90 seconds to 120 seconds. However, this varies considerably from athlete to athlete. May be easier to take pulse.

Lesser trained   = 100-120 beats/minute
Advanced trained = 125-135 beats/minute

4. Duration

- In the running athlete duration ranges from about 15 seconds for 100 meters to about 85-90 seconds for 400m and, of course, will vary when compared to other sports.

Intensive Work

1. Intensity

- Relatively a high or intensive. As running intensity between 80-90% but as strength exercise usually 75% of maximum capacity.

2. Volume

Because intensity of action is increased the repetitions are usually much lower in number. Exhaustion still comes gradually. After the "recovery break" fatigue still is evident when next repeat is started. During series break (recovery-rest) the fatigue factor does lower.

3. Density

- This is high intensity so "break" is much longer ($1^{1}/_{2}$-3 minutes, advanced athletes, and beginners 2-4 minutes). Pulse rate = 120-135 and 100-200 for beginners.

4. Duration

- Short exercise of 80-90% maximum lasts about 50-70 seconds. Strength exercises about 75% maximum and duration increased by greater load. Usually done at high speed for 8-10 reps. and perhaps in 1-3 series.

Pulse Rate

1. Immediately after end of exercise.
2. Immediately after the break or recovery rest.

Repetition Exercise

1. Intensity

- Exercise at very high intensity. Approximately 80-100% of maximum. Strength 80-90%.

2. Volume

- Repetitions are low in number. Usually 2-6 (the likes of runners) and 3-6 lifts per series for barbell lifts, or 20-35 lifts in total unit.

3. Density

- Long break (rest) after each effort of about 3-4 + minutes or with the barbell 2-3 minutes.

4. Duration

Variable length of training from 2 seconds to 6 or 10 minutes. Strength training always only 1 second.

This type of exercise gives strong nerve and muscle interactions. Improves:

1. Speed
2. Maximum strength
3. Speed endurance.

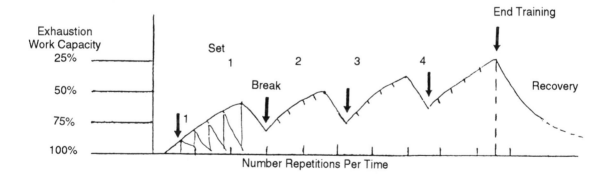

DO MIDDLE DISTANCE RUNNERS NEED STRENGTH?

by V. Gertmanets, Y. Travin, USSR

Overrating the importance of strength training in long distance running can be as harmful as underrating it. In the following text the authors explain how an improved muscular power output can reduce the energy expenditure in the mechanical work of running and outline how to structure an efficient strength development program for middle distance running.

Until recently experts divided strength into the components of maximum (absolute) strength, relative strength (absolute strength per kilogram of body weight), power (speed strength) and strength endurance. Modern research has isolated an additional component in the ability of a muscle to develop energy from elastic deformation.

This ability explains the metabolic efficiency of running with a reduced outlay of mechanical work. The muscles and connecting tendons develop potential energy during the eccentric (yielding) work phase to utilize it during the concentric (overcoming) work phase, exploiting non-metabolic energy. The use of non-metabolic energy during a muscle contraction occurs directly after the preliminary stretching of the muscle, thus reducing the energy expenditure needed for the mechanical work.

In middle distance running the energy expenditure to complete one running stride is 1.5 kilojoules and the work is performed using the athlete's strength capacities in two phases—the eccentric and the concentric. The muscles of the support leg operate in the eccentric phase, that occupies 15 to 20% of the total running stride from the moment the foot strikes the track until it reaches the vertical position. This is followed by the concentric phase which makes up about 30 to 35% of the running stride and lasts from the vertical position until the foot breaks contact with the track.

As the athlete's performance level improves, a decrease of the total muscular contraction time is observed. The relaxation time is now increased by 40 to 60%, showing that the improved power output of the contractions produces the same work in less time.

METHODS AND MEANS

Long distance runners develop strength while running. However, athletes can significantly improve their strength development by performing specific exercises. Many studies have shown that a properly structured strength training program increases the effectiveness of the entire training plan.

Specific strength training has a strong influence, not only on the muscular strength level, but also on the neuromuscular system, adaptation to endurance work and the exploitation of the body's functional reserves. The intra-muscular energy potential is elevated, oxidative processes improved and the blood supply to the working muscles increased.

Specific exercises, which involve more intensive work than in competitive running, are among the fundamental methods in the training of long distance runners and include the following:

- Running in harder than normal conditions (sand, snow, water)
- Hill running at a moderate pace with frequent accelerations
- Interval sprint training
- Running with weighted resistances, such as a weight belt, heavy running shoes, pulling a car tire and so on
- Uphill bounding
- One-legged and two-legged multiple hops and bounding from one leg to the other
- Static muscle contractions at joint angles that correspond approximately to running action angles
- Specific strength development exercises with free weights and other training aids.

Assisting exercises are included for general strength development, involving muscle groups that are not the prime movers in the running action.

The fundamental principle in the selection of strength development means is their dynamic similarity to the muscle contractions that occur in the competitive event. This means that specific strength training exercises should reflect the same type of muscle contractions and movement dynamics as in racing.

The effectiveness of specific strength training is governed by the appropriate selection of the exercises and the conditions in which they are performed. Thus, the type of muscular work, the amount of resistance, the tempo, the number of repetitions, the duration and nature of recoveries and the total number of exercises performed in a training session determine the results.

THE STRUCTURE OF STRENGTH TRAINING

Strength training in distance running is not a new "in" approach. It is a well-known fact that athletes used strength methods extensively in the late 50's and early 60's. Accordingly, it is wiser to discuss an efficient scheduling of strength training in the year's cycle, rather than its advantages and disadvantages.

The recommendations presented in this text have been tested in a study of higher level endurance athletes, whose individual strength components were developed and monitored by using diagnostic tests. Consequently, the following should present a most effective plan for the structuring of specific strength training.

Stage 1—Begins at the start of the preparation period and lasts 60 to 80 days. The aim is to improve the relative strength of the thigh and lower leg flexors and extensors to 120-125% and strength endurance to 130-140%. The test results during the transition period are taken as 100%.

Stage 2—Takes place in the middle of the preparation period and lasts 25 to 30 days. The aim is to lift the level of strength endurance to 220-240% and at the same time maintain the relative strength so that it does not drop below the level of 112-115%.

Stage 3—Takes place during the winter competition period and lasts 25 to 30 days. The aim is to maintain the level of strength endurance at the 240% mark, while the relative strength should remain around 110-115%. At the same time the development of energy from elastic deformation should be increased to 130-150%.

Stage 4—This takes place at the end of the preparation period and lasts 50 to 60 days. The aim is to improve the level of relative strength to 120-125% and strength endurance to 250-280%.

Stage 5—This covers the pre-competition period and lasts 25 to 30 days. The aim is to raise the level of strength endurance to 300-350%, to increase the muscular elastic deformation energy to 130-140% and at the same time maintain the relative strength level to around 115-120%.

Stage 6—The competition season, lasting 120 to 150 days. The aim is to maintain the level of strength endurance at 250-300%, the level of relative strength at 108-115% and the capacity of the elastic deformation energy at 140-150%.

THE TRAINING MEANS

The development of the individual strength components takes place by using the following main training means:

1. Leg presses or barbell squats. The resistance is adjusted so that the athlete can perform 5 to 8 repetitions with 80 to 90% of maximum effort. The weight is lowered half as fast as it is lifted. One training session includes 4 to 5 sets with 8 to 10 minute recoveries between the sets. Flexibility and relaxation exercises are performed during the recoveries.

This exercise is used mainly in the first and fourth stages to develop relative strength and inter-muscular coordination of the slow twitch muscle fibers. Stage 1 includes 20 to 24 workouts, stage 2 only four, stage 3 two, and stage 4 about 25 workouts. The exercise is not used during stages 5 and 6. A restorative cross country run is recommended following the strength training session.

2. Leg flexion and hip and knee extension. The exercises are performed in the following sequence:

* Standing on one leg—the extension of the other leg against resistance

* Standing facing gymnastic wall bars—the backward extension of the thigh against a resisting device (rubber or spring)

* Lying in prone position—the flexing of the knee

joint against a resisting device (rubber or spring)

This group of exercises is performed in combination with leg presses or barbell squats. The number of repetitions, sets and recoveries are the same as in exercise group 1.

3. *The same exercises as in groups 1 and 2* with a resistance 60 to 70% of the maximum, employing 65 to 80 repetitions. The exercises are performed rapidly, using 2 to 3 sets in a single workout. Recoveries are adjusted according to the heart rate, expected to drop to 80 to 90 beats/min. before the next set is started.

The number of workouts: stage 1-25, stage 2-80, stage 3-40, stage 4-30, stage 5-12 and stage 6-30.

4. *Uphill bounding* (35° angle) is conducted over 150 to 400m distances 2 or 3 times a week. The recoveries last until the heart rate drops to 110 to 130 beats/min. The number of repetitions in a set ranges from 5 to 6 and an average workout includes 5 to 6 sets. One workout totals 5 to 6km.

The exercise is first used in stage 4 (15 to 20 times), followed by 3 to 4 times in stage 5 and 8 to 10 times in stage 6.

5. *Multiple hops, medicine ball throws and rapid squat jumps* with a partner on shoulders are performed all year round during the final stages of the warm-up. The most common are "long" multiple hops. 8 series over 150m.

6. *Static exercises* are usually performed during the recovery pauses between interval sprints. These exercises involve leg flexion and extension at the hip, knee and ankle joints against static resistance. The joint angles should correspond to the primary angles in the running action. Static exercises are employed in stages 2, 3 and 5.

7. *Accelerations* of 6 to 8 seconds every 2 to 3 minutes in moderate aerobic running are used all year round. One workout is usually made up from 5 to 12 accelerations. The number of workouts: stage 1-20, stage 2-15, stage 3-12, stage 4-8, stage 5-12, stage 6-40.

Considering the total time of the seven exercise groups as 100% allows the establishment of month by month distribution percentages as follows: October—10%, November—20%, December—7%, January—4%, February—3%, March—22%, April—5%, May—4%, June—10%, July to September—5%.

TESTING

Systematic monitoring of the developmental level of specific strength components must take place by employing on-going weekly tests (after a rest day) and stage tests (4 to 5 times a year). The following simple tests are recommended:

- Strength endurance is evaluated by the number of leg presses or barbell squats with a weight 50% of the maximum. The legs are bent 80 to 90% at the knee and hip joints

- Absolute strength of the leg extensors is decided by the maximum weights lifted in the leg press or barbell squat. The fraction derived from dividing the absolute strength by the body weight establishes relative strength

- The capacity of the muscles to accumulate energy from elastic deformation is based on the difference between the standing vertical jump with a three-second pause and without a pause

- Speed strength is evaluated by the height achieved in the standing vertical jump.

IN CONCLUSION

In summary it must be stressed that the development of the various strength capacities is not an end in itself! Strength is only a component of the total training process of a middle distance runner. Overrating the importance of strength training, or structuring it improperly, is just as harmful as underrating its value.

THE FEMALE ENDURANCE RUNNER

by Norman D. Brook, Great Britain

British AAB coach Brook catalogs the physical differences between men and women insofar as endurance running is concerned, but stresses that the training load and intensity level can be the same for women as for men.

Women distance runners can train as hard as men; however, there are a number of structural, anatomical and physiological differences which lead to performance variation, due mainly to differences in the aerobic performance capacity and strength.

Women's distance running events were reluctantly included in the Olympics for the first time in 1928 at the Amsterdam Games. The longest event was the 800m which was won by Lina Radke of Germany in 2 minutes 16.8 seconds. Unfortunately, few of the competitors in this event had ever tried the distance before and as a result they finished the race in considerable distress. The scene of several women collapsing with exhaustion at the finish of the race lead to an outcry from the press who complained of the folly of women running so far. The outcome of these complaints was the removal of the 800m from the Olympic program for 32 years. It wasn't until 1960 that the 800m was reintroduced and it was another 12 years before the 1500m was introduced. The introduction of the 3000m showed that it was slowly becoming accepted that women could take part in endurance running events.

Attitudes towards women taking part in endurance running events have gradually changed. There is, however, still a lingering notion that women are not as suited to endurance running as their male counterparts and this is often evident from the approach of some female endurance runners and their coaches towards training. Women now take part in events from 800m to the marathon and beyond, yet there are still those who think that women cannot train as hard as men. This just isn't true; women *can* train as hard as men.

Female runners may not run as fast or complete the same volume of training as their male compatriots. However, when it comes to effort and time spent in training their contributions are similar.

Although it is a fact that there are performance related differences between the genders, these do not extend to the amount of hard work that needs to be done to be a successful endurance athlete, as this component is the same for both sexes.

MALE/FEMALE DIFFERENCES

There are a number of structural, anatomical and physiological differences between the sexes which lead to performance variations between men and women in the endurance events. Despite these differences there are as many similarities between the sexes which explain the considerable overlap between the ranges of performance in men and women. Even though the best male endurance runners are faster than the best female runners, the best women run much faster than most men.

Performance differences between the male and female runners can be explained by the influence of structural, anatomical and physiological factors on aerobic endurance and strength.

AEROBIC ENDURANCE

Maximal oxygen uptake, taken as an absolute value, before being divided by the athlete's body weight, is substantially lower in women than in men. Absolute VO_2 max for the average female is only 40-60% of that of the average male. When bodyweight is taken into consideration and the relative value is calculated, the difference is reduced to 20-30% of that of the average male. Much of the difference in absolute VO_2 max is due to the female's smaller physique. If VO_2 max is compared with lean body mass and the body's stores of adipose tissue are ignored, the difference is further reduced to 15%. This shows that the lower relative maximum oxygen uptake is partly due to the higher percentage of body fat in female runners. The percentage of body fat in men in the general population ranges from 10.9-22.3% and for women the range is 21.9-29.8%. Male endurance runners are often measured with less than 10% body fat while percentages for female runners tend to be around 10-13%.

A factor which influences VO_2 max is the blood's ability to transport oxygen around the body. Hemoglobin, which is contained in the red blood cells, carries the oxygen from the lungs to the muscles. The average male has about 6% more hemoglobin. A pint of blood from a women will not have the potential to carry as much oxygen as a pint of blood from a man. However, it is thought that there are higher concentrations of 2,3 DPG in the hemoglobin of women which will partly offset the lower hemoglobin concentrations. The lower hemoglobin and the fact that women have a lower total volume of blood explain why women have a lower oxygen carrying potential.

Another important factor influencing VO_2 max is the rate at which blood is pumped around the body. This is determined by the athlete's cardiac output, which is the product of the working heart rate and the heart's stroke volume. There is no difference between working heart rates in men and women, so any difference in cardiac output is due to stroke volume. Men have on average an absolute cardiac output which is 40% better than that of women. When bodyweight is taken into consideration, the female has a cardiac output which is 80-90% of that of the male.

The ability of the muscles to extract oxygen from the bloodstream is a third factor which influences maximal oxygen uptake. Oxygen is extracted from the blood by myoglobin and is utilized in cells called mitochondria.

The amount of myoglobin and number of mitochondria are lower in women than in men and the density of oxidative enzymes in the female's mitochondria is lower than in men. This reduces the female's ability to extract oxygen and together with their lower oxygen transporting capacity contributes to the 15% difference in maximal oxygen uptake between the sexes.

Maximum oxygen uptake is an important factor in endurance events. However, the longer the event the more important the anaerobic threshold, the percentage of maximum oxygen uptake that can be utilized without significant increase in the blood lactate levels. When expressed as a percentage of VO_2 max there is no difference in anaerobic threshold between the sexes. However, the female runner has a lower VO_2 max and therefore she must have a lower absolute anaerobic threshold.

STRENGTH

Strength levels in women are lower by 55-80% than in men due partly to women possessing less muscle mass. Muscle only accounts for about 35.8% of total bodyweight in women, compared with 41.8% in men. While they have a lower muscle mass than men they have the same number of muscle fibers. The muscle fibers in women are of a smaller cross-sectional area due to the lower plasma testosterone levels, the hormone which encourages muscle hypertrophy. Training will produce similar relative strength gains in men and women. Women will, however, not increase total body weight significantly as there will be considerably less muscle hypertrophy due to hormonal differences between the sexes.

Women have lower levels of strength which influence performance in endurance events by preventing the development of an economical running action and the ability to sprint or change pace. Strength can be improved through training without the worry of increasing muscle mass.

ANAEROBIC ENDURANCE

When it comes to the anaerobic energy systems, there are no differences between the sexes. The effects of anaerobic training and the acquired ability to tolerate the build-up of lactic acid are not sex dependent. There may, however, be some variation in lactate production during the menstrual cycle with improved anaerobic performance during the luteal phase.

RUNNING EFFICIENCY

The energy costs of running at set speeds may be higher in female athletes due to a reduced running efficiency caused by the female structure. Differences in the female anatomy also mean a lesser ability to sprint and change pace. The average female is smaller by about 5 inches and lighter by about 30-40 pounds than the average male. She has about 10% more body fat, much of which is deposited around the thighs and buttocks lowering her center of gravity. The wider pelvis, slanting of the thighs towards the knees, narrower shoulders, and shorter limbs in relation to her body length, all influence the running mechanics of women.

While a woman's lower level of functional strength will have a negative influence on the development of sprinting speed, their better mobility and coordination levels are positive factors.

REPRODUCTION FUNCTION

Endurance training has been associated with a number of changes which happen in the menstrual cycle of female runners. Young female runners engaging in serious endurance training before puberty may have their menarche delayed until their late teens and are likely to develop a long, lithe figure. The female who takes up serious endurance training in her early twenties may be vulnerable to exercise-induced or secondary amenorrhea. These changes are associated with lower basal estrogen and are reversible when training ceases.

If the runner wishes to control her fertility she may need to consider birth control methods. Contraceptive options are the oral contraceptive, intrauterine devices, barrier methods, rhythm method and abstinence. While the birth control pill is a convenient form of contraception, it is not popular among endurance runners. Although there are a number of positive aspects associated with the pill, including the predictable menstrual cycle, the negative aspects may affect performance. Women athletes taking the pill have experienced a significant reduction in the oxygen uptake. There is also the possibility of increased percentage of body fat, which would result in a decrease in relative VO_2 max. After ceasing the pill, VO_2 max should return to normal within six weeks.

Intrauterine devices are not a popular form of contraception with athletic women. Barrier methods are, as they are only used when needed, have little or no risks and, when used properly together with spermicidal jelly, compare well with the effectiveness of the oral contraceptive.

The rhythm method presents problems for the female runner due to the alterations which occur with the menstrual cycle as a result of endurance training. Irregular cycles or rapid reversing of amenorrhea make this method of birth control unreliable. Abstinence is the most reliable method and in the serious runner this may become easier when training is intense, the goals that are being worked for are important, and if she has no regular partner.

During menstruation hemoglobin levels may fall leaving the female athlete anemic. Normal hemoglobin concentration tests may show the athlete to have below-normal levels but this may be due to the increased blood volume caused by training. To check if the female athlete is anemic it is important to measure serum ferritin levels which correlate with the body's total iron stores.

IMPLICATIONS FOR TRAINING

Women can train as hard as men and if they wish to reach the highest levels of participation they must be prepared to spend the same amount of time in training as would elite men. Their training loads will be at the same intensity and involve a similar volume of training to those of men with equivalent best performances. Any difference in training loads will be related to performance level rather than gender. The methods used in training and the annual training plans are the same as those for men. Within the annual training plan, more attention may be devoted to the development of aerobic endurance and strength, as women are weaker in these areas of conditioning. However, this should not detract from other important aspects of training.

Women may need to supplement iron and vitamin C as they are prone to anemia at certain stages of the menstrual cycle. A doctor with an interest in sport should be asked to monitor hemoglobin levels and to prescribe iron therapy if required. It may also be advisble to supplement the B complex vitamins which are involved in energy metabolism, especially if the runner is using oral contraceptives. Some runners and the parents of young female runners may be concerned at the loss of menstrual periods associated with endurance training. In such cases the runner should consult her doctor, who may refer her to a specialist who in turn can conduct tests to confirm that the loss of periods is due to the training load and will be restored when training ceases.

Some female runners tend to worry about their weight and are not always sensible in weight control practices. It may be necessary to recruit the services of a dietician who can advise on diet and weight control. Percentage of body fat and weight are useful measures to keep throughout the training year to help ensure that the runner reaches her optimal relative maximum oxygen uptake.

OVERTRAINING AND THE ROLE OF PHARMACOLOGY

by Dr. Kaidu Meitern, Estonia

Dr. Kaidu Meitern, who is the medical adviser of the Estonian Republic's track team, looks at the problems and symptoms of overtraining and the role of pharmaceutical aids to secure restoration after heavy workloads.

ABOUT OVERTRAINING

The volume and intensity of training continue to increase and are responsible for the improvement of performances. Athletes often attempt to copy the number of training sessions, the duration of workouts and other indicators related to the training of top level performers, overlooking the fact that all athletes don't tolerate similar training loads. The organism can easily be overloaded when inherited characteristics and the prerequisites to lift the training load are not taken into consideration.

Finnish sport physiologist V. Harkonen defines overtraining as a state where, despite intensive training, the work capacity of an athlete fails to improve, or even drops. West German sport medicine specialist W. Kindermann claims that "overtraining is reflected in a drop of performance capacities, in the absence of illness, of an athlete who trains regularly. It is expressed in modest subjective and objective symptoms."

What leads to overtraining? The inherited capacity to tolerate certain workloads has already been mentioned. The most common additional reasons are:

- Incorrect training methods, frequently including a monotonous and rapidly increased training volume. Most often, however, it is the intensity of a forced training load that is responsible for more damage than a large volume
- Training while ill, or training immediately after an illness
- Work or study loads and stresses that coincide with hard training
- Psychological problems.

Table 1: Overload Symptoms

Symptomatic	Parasymptomatic
Easily fatigued	Easily fatigued
irritation	calmness
poor sleep	normal sleep
lack of appetite	normal appetite
loss of weight	no changes in weight
Easy sweating	Normal sweating
Sweating in sleep	—
Frequent headaches	No headaches
Fast resting pulse	Normal resting pulse
Light fever (99°)	Normal body temperature
Faster metabolism	—
Poor recovery after a workload	—
Higher breathing frequency	Normal breathing
Poor toleration to stress	—
Disturbances in movement coordination	Poor coordination under heavy workloads
Shorter reaction time	Normal or lengthened reaction time
Restless or depressed mood	Normal mood

How is it possible to anticipate overtraining? There are two main categories of overtraining. The first, the symptomatic category, is easier to diagnose because the symptoms are typical and disturb mainly the inner feelings of an athlete. It affects mainly beginners, young athletes and participants in the non-endurance events. The second, the para-symptomatic category, has less obvious symptoms and is far more difficult to forestall. It occurs usually among endurance athletes and older performers. Table 1 presents a summary of the main overtraining symptoms in both categories.

The athlete must take notice of any changes in his condition and contact a doctor at the first sign of abnormal fatigue, a drop in performance capacities, or any of the listed symptoms. The doctor, in turn, has to establish whether the symptoms indicate organic illness or one caused by functional disturbances from overtraining.

EVALUATION METHODS

Reasonably simple and objective methods to evaluate overtraining are the resting pulse rate and changes in the body weight. Medical examinations can naturally provide a far more reliable diagnosis by comparing changes in the pulse rate, blood pressure and ECG in lying down and standing positions. An increase in the pulse rate by more than 25 beats a minute, a drop of the systolic blood pressure over 20 mmHg and T-inversions on the cardiograph are typical symptoms of overloading.

The above-mentioned simple tests do not provide sufficient information in high performance sport where we are dealing with parasymptomatic changes. Biochemical laboratory tests, such as establishing changes in the hemoglobin concentration (drops under overloading), are needed.

The establishment of the hormonal status of the organism, because of the important function of endogen hormones in the metabolism of proteins, has for some time been employed to discover overtraining. Under normal conditions there is a balance in the operation of catabolic and anabolic hormones. A change in the balance can be caused by overloading the organism. There are two possibilities to maintain the hormonal balance in intensive training. Training loads can be moderately reduced to find an optimal load, or they can be continued under a controlled intake of anabolic steroids. The latter is, of course, illegal and at present prohibited.

Overtraining can also be diagnosed by regularly checking blood lactate concentrations. Theory and practical experience indicates that overtraining is reflected in a low maximal blood lactate level.

All the above-mentioned biochemical tests help to discover an already established overtraining status. Overtraining can, however, be forestalled by observing the athlete's urea concentration, which informs us about the catabolic metabolism in the organism. This concentration increases steadily under heavy training loads but should not exceed 50 mg%.

The continuous chase of new records requires further increases in the intensity and volume of training. This, in turn, requires improved restoration methods to avoid overtraining syndromes and has in contemporary sport led to the use of pharmacology.

PHARMACOLOGY HAS A PLACE IN SPORT

Pharmacology and sport—these two words are usually related to the abuse of prohibited substances with the aim of improving performances. However, pharmacology plays in sport another, far more deserving, role in forestalling and preventing the overloading of the organism and its functional systems.

In our contemporary approach we have to look to the past and think of the future. In doing so we can see that pharmacology has forced its way into sport with the same momentum as professionalism. The use of new pharmaceutical substances and preparations is increasing rapidly and it appears doubtful that this boom is going to stop. Professionalism in sport simply demands a maximal exploitation of all potentialities.

Keep in mind, for example, that the pulse frequency in some sporting activities reaches 200 to 230 beats a minute, systolic blood pressure in the effort phase in weightlifting can reach over 300 to 350 mmHg (normally 100 to 140 mmHg), interval training frequently takes place in an extremely high oxygen debt situation, the liver is often in what can be called as a disturbed state in heavy training phases and so on. There is no doubt that such extreme situations require far more than just a few words from the doctor.

There are many pharmaceutical treatments and restorative substances available for use in sport. The number of allowable substances exceeds several times the approximately 800 banned doping preparations. The use of the non-prohibited pharmaceutical substances is, as already mentioned, closely related to the use of large and very large training loads. The aim is to:

- Prevent and treat various overtraining syndromes

- Prevent the overloading of single organs and functional systems
- Maintain the work capacity of an athlete, and
- Speed up recovery processes.

RECOVERY PROCESSES

The recovery capacity from heavy workloads and the adaptation to them are the main prerequisites for high level performances in contemporary sport. The regulation of recovery processes is therefore looked upon as the biological means to maintain a homogeneous balance in the organism and to improve at a certain performance level or age the athlete's adaptation capacity (D. Davidenko).

Obviously, the planning of training processes under these circumstances cannot take place without taking recovery into consideration. The pharmaceutical substances that assist recovery, according to the weaknesses of the organism, can be classified as follows:

- Preparations that coordinate and stimulate the nervous system
- Preparations that correct the functioning of the cardiovascular sytem and improve the quality of blood
- Preparations that protect the liver and activate its functions
- Preparations that regulate metabolism
- Vitamins.

Pharmaceutically assisted corrections to prevent overtraining require close cooperation between the doctor, the coach and the athlete. By taking into consideration changes in the work capacity of an athlete, the restoration following certain workloads and complex biochemical indicators, it is possible to speed up recovery immediately after a workout, as well as after longer training periods. Favorable conditions can consequently be created for the employment of high training loads.

The use of pharmaceutical restoration substances in sport can naturally create complicated social and ethical problems. For example, does the use of such substances give one athlete an unfair advantage over another? On the other hand, we know well that far more important physical advantages, given by nature to some athletes, are never considered.

As it stands, there also is no exact knowledge of the effect of pharmaceutical preparations used for recovery and restoration, although some research has gone into establishment of the dynamics of pharmaceutical substances in the adaptation to large training loads. There is a lack of exact and concrete indicators.

Nevertheless, the use of pharmacological preparations in sport is necessary, particularly when large or extremely large training loads are employed. It is important in order to maintain a homogeneous balance in the organism and to treat the syndrome of strain which is, after all, the same pathological condition as any other illness.

CHAPTER II

SPECIFIC CONCEPTS

THE SCIENTIFIC BASES OF TRAINING FOR MIDDLE DISTANCE RUNNING

by William Black, USA

A well documented summary of physiological factors and their contributions to the performance of middle distance running that determine the choice of individual training means and methods.

Performance in any athletic event is a result of the interaction of several factors, each of which makes a relative contribution. Thayer (1980) identified four broad categories affecting performance as:

1. Physical
2. Psychological
3. Technical
4. Tactical

This study will address only the physical aspects of middle distance running and attempt to provide information that can be applied to the formulation of training programs to improve the middle distance running performance. Of course, not all of the possible factors from any of the four broad categories that can contribute to athletic performance make a significant contribution to a specific sport or specialty within a sport. For example, in track and field, the factors that significantly contribute to pole vaulting success are considerably different than those that make an outstanding 10,000 meter runner, which are considerably different than those that make a successful discus thrower. Oftentimes the differences are obvious but in those cases where the demands of the event are similar, the differences between being a champion athlete and an also-ran are difficult to identify. For example, Pollock and co-investigators (1980) were able to identify physiological differences between elite and good long distance (5000 meters-marathon) runners, but these same characteristics could not discriminate between the elite 5,000-10,000 meter runners and the elite marathoners. It was necessary for them to identify a second set of variables in order to differentiate between the two groups of elite runners. The significance of the differences is great.

Knowing what factors contribute to better performance makes it possible to:

1. Design training programs that will stress the factors the athlete needs most to be successful.
2. Avoid doing unnecessary training. Identifying the factors (absolute speed, anaerobic power, aerobic capacity, flexibility, etc.) that contribute to success in any athletic activity requires that:

   1. The nature and demands of the activity be identified.
   2. The physical and physiological characteristics of all levels of participants be identified.

Acccurate interpretation of the information will make it possible to:

1. Determine what physical and physiological characteristics are necessary to perform at a particular level.
2. Determine the best training methods to improve performance.

NATURE AND DEMANDS OF MIDDLE DISTANCE RUNNING

In this report, middle distance running will be defined as the 800, 1500, and 3000m races as contested in standard track competition. Depending on the level of competition, the duration of effort in middle distance racing ranges from slightly under 1 minute and 42 seconds to approximately 11 minutes.

• McArdle and co-investigators (1967) reported mean heart rates of 186, 195 and 206 beats per minute for contestants in 880 yards, mile, and 2-

mile races.

The greatest lactate acidosis with pH values of under 6.9 and lactate levels up to 25 mmol/l were found in the runners under acute physiological stress for 1-2 minutes (400, 500 and 800m running).

- Kindermann and Keul (1977) reported a pH of 6.892 after an 800m run in 1:49.5.
- Osnes and Hermansen (1972) reported blood lactate levels following an 800m run in 1:50.8 and a 1500m run in 3:48.0 of slightly less than 20 mmol/l and slightly less than 25 mmol/l, respectively.
- Svedenhag and Sjodin (1984) reported blood lactate concentrations of 15.7 and 16.2 mmol/l taken one minute after major competition in 800m and 1500m runners, respectively. Three minutes after competition the blood lactate levels in each group were 18.4 mmol/l.
- Kindermann and Keul (1977) reported a significant reduction in lactate concentration and a significant increase in pH between the 1500m and 3000m steeplechase runs for male track athletes participating in international competition.

This information, of course, indicates that there is considerable involvement of the anaerobic glycolytic energy producing system during middle distance running competition, and that the shorter the distance, the greater the involvement of anaerobic energy sources.

- According to Kindermann and Keul (1977), energy production for the 800m run is supplied 50% by anaerobic metabolism and 50% by aerobic metabolism, while "aerobic production clearly predominates in the case of a 1500m run."
- Gladrow (1983) states that for the 800, 1500, and 3000m runs the aerobic/anaerobic energy production ratios are 34/66, 50/50, and 75/25, respectively.
- Ovishinnikov and Ilyev reported that, of the factors that contribute to performance in the 800 and 1500m runs, the most important are, in order:

(1) Anaerobic capacity, 43.65 to 800 and 37.4% to 1500m performance.
(2) Aerobic capacity, 23.5% to 800 and 29.5% to 1500m performance.
(3) Aerobic efficiency contributes 17.1% to 800m performance, and
(4) Speed and power contribute 12.6% to 1500m

performance.

- Similar findings are reported by Berg and Bell (1980) in a study to identify the determinants of performance for the mile run.

Analysis of world-class (and former world record) runs of 1:43.4 and 3:32.2 showed that the runners ran 380.9 and 750 strides at average velocities of 7.07 and 6.31 m/sec., respectively. The runners had mean stride lengths of 2.1 and 2.0 meters and mean stride frequencies of 3.67 and 3.53/10m (Scholick, 1978).

PROGRESSIVE CHANGES IN PHYSIOLOGICAL CHARACTERISTICS AS A RESULT OF TRAINING AND COMPETITION

Periodic testing of high-level middle distance runners over the course of a year determined that several changes took place which contributed to improved running performance. They were:

1. Increased maximum oxygen uptake relative to bodyweight (expressed in ml/kg/min.)
2. Increased blood lactate concentration after exhaustion.
3. Increased running velocity corresponding to a blood lactate concentration of 4 mmol/l.
4. Decreased oxygen consumption at submaximum running speed (increased running economy).
5. Decreased bodyfat (which contributes to an increased maximum oxygen uptake per kilogram of bodyweight). Conley, et al., 1984; Svedenhag & Sjodin, 1985.

- Wyndham and co-researchers (1969) noted that, during the early stages of training, a sub-four minute miler, while performing a treadmill test had increased lactic acid concentrations at about 60% of his maximum oxygen uptake at that time and that, after he had reached a high state of competitive fitness, the lactic acid concentration increased at about 67% of his maximum oxygen uptake at that time. Additionally, the concentrations of lactic acid were much lower, even at a higher level of oxygen consumption, while in a highly trained state than in the early stages of training.
- Conley, Krahenbuhl, and Burkett (1981) found that during the training of an elite distance runner, "most of the improvements in running economy were noted during or immediately after weeks of increased interval training."
- Anderson, Lamb, and Maestas (1986) tested

twelve intercollegiate cross-country runners during thirteen weeks of training and found that the greatest gains in running economy occurred in the first six weeks of training when training consisted of significantly more distance running and less interval running than during the second six weeks of training. They concluded that "the results do not appear to support previous findings which have reported gains in RE (running economy) as a result of increased amounts of interval training."

ANAEROBIC CAPACITY

• Schnabel and Kindermann (1983) reported a non-statistically significant tendency for a lower time to exhaustion (83 vs. 88 seconds), and arterial blood lactate levels 17.5 vs. 16.3 mmol/l for middle disance runners, as compared to 400m runners, following runs leading to exhaustion in approximately 1 minute and 25 seconds.

These values were significantly higher than those for long distance and marathon runners, indicating a greater anaerobic capacity and glycolytic energy expenditure for the 400m and middle distance runners.

• McKenzie, Parkhouse and Hearst (1982) reported a mean time to exhaustion of 114 seconds and post test blood lactate concentrations of 22 mmol/l. upon performance of the Anaerobic Speed Test (treadmill run at 3.52 m/sec., 20 degrees incline) for a group of middle distance runners, compared to a mean time to exhaustion of 54 seconds for marathon runners.
• Elite Canadian soccer players were able to run for a mean time of 92.5 seconds (Rhodes, et al., 1986).

AEROBIC POWER

Various studies reported maximum oxygen uptakes in the high 60's (expressed in ml/kg/min.) for middle distance runners, which are significantly lower than the maximum oxygen uptake values in the 70's of long distance runners, and higher than the values in the 50's achieved by sprinters (Barnes, 1981: Boileau, et al., 1982; Crielaard and Pirnay, 1981; Komi, et al., 1977: Rusko, et al., 1978: Thomas, et al., 1983).

ANAEROBIC POWER

Male middle distance runners had reported

mean Margaria test scores of 1.40 and 1.45 m/sec. Women runners scored 1.28 m/sec. The men's scores compare to mean scores of 1.57 m/sec. for power (sprints, throws, jumps) athletes, 1.51 m/sec. for power (sprints, throws, jumps) athletes, 1.51 m/sec. for Finnish physical education students, and 1.31 m/sec. for long distance runners. (Bosco, et al., 1980: Komi, et al., 1977). Female softball, netball, and field hockey athletes achieved mean scores of 1.28, 1.31, and 1.33 m/sec., respectively (Withers and Roberts, 1981).

• Taunton, Maron and Wilkinson (1981) reported Margaria Test scores of 109.6 and 109.5 kg/m/sec. for middle and long distance runners, respectively.
• The 800m and long distance runners tested by Komi and co-researchers (1977) achieved 101.8 kg/m/sec. and 87.1 kg/m/sec., respectively.
• Withers, Roberts, and Davies (1977) reported a score of 115.8 kg/m/sec. for a runner capable of running the 800m in 1:49.4.
• Mean scores achieved by male basketball, field hockey, and soccer players were 120.45, 115.5, and 125.9 kg/m/sec. respectively (Withers, et al., 1977).

DISCUSSION

Research shows that several physiological factors contribute to middle distance running performance. Among those identified are:

1. Anaerobic capacity.
2. Aerobic power.
3. Running economy (the percentage of maximum oxygen uptake used at submaximum speed).
4. Anaerobic power.

Knowing what qualities are needed for successful performance, the relative contribution of each quality, and the level of performance needed for each to run at a particular level makes it possible to:

1. Choose the proper training means and methods.
2. Organize them into an effective system of training.

For example, it has been determined that the runner's time for the 400m dash, which requires a great anaerobic capacity, has the closest correlation with 800m running performance and that particular 400m performance levels correspond with particular 800m performance levels. There is the same correlation between ability in the 3000m run, which requires a high aerobic power, and ability in the 1500m run and between particular levels of ability in each (Nurmekivi, 1985).

However, while available knowledge indicates what qualities contribute to middle distance running performance, there is a lack of information regarding the most effective system of training to enable the athlete to realize his/her potential because of the possibility that there is more than one type of athlete capable of achieving a high level in middle distance running. Apparently not addressed by scientific research is the concept that there are two or three types of 800m runners whose differing physiological characteristics enable them to perform at the same level as the result of differing relative contributions of the factors that affect performance (Vanden Eynde, 1985; Karikosk, 1958). According to Karikosk, each type of runner will perform better if he/she trains with the method best suited to his/her physiological makeup. Recently, credence has been lent to this concept by the fact that a non-traditional training program has been formulated on the national level to train 400m runners to compete in the 800 meters (Krukssman and Schmidt, 1985), as well as the fact that performances on the highest levels have been achieved by runners using varying training methods.

REFERENCES

Anderson, M.B., J.L. Lamb, and R.W. Maestas; "Changes in Running Economy in Cross Country Runners", International Journal of Sports Medicine, 1986, 7; p. 177 (abstract).

Berg, K. and C.W. Bell, "Physiological and Anthropometric Determinants of Mile Run Time", Journal of Sports Medicine and Physical Fitness, 20, 1980; pp. 390-96.

Boileau, R.A., J.L. Mayhew, W.F. Riner and L. Lussier, "Physiological Characteristics of Elite Middle and Long Distance Runners", Canadian Journal of Applied Sport Sciences, 1982; 7(3); pp. 167-72.

Bosco, C., P.V. Komi and K. Sinkkonen, "Mechanical Power, Net Efficiency and Muscle Structure in Male and Female Middle Distance Runners", Scandinavian Journal of Sports Sciences, 1980; 2(2); pp. 47-51.

Carter, J., F.W. Kasch, J.L. Boyer, W.H. Phillips, M.D. Ross and A. Sucec, "Structural and Functional Assessments on a Champion Runner—Peter Snell", Research Quarterly, 1967; 38(3); pp. 355-65.

Conley, D., G. Krahenbuhl, L.N. Burket, and A.L. Millar, "Following Steve Scott: Physiological Changes Accompanying Training", The Physician and Sportsmedicine, Jan., 1984; 12(1).

Costill, D.L., D.S. King, R. Thomas and M. Hargreaves, "Effects of Reduced Training on Muscular Power in Swimmers," The Physician and Sportsmedicine, Feb. 1985; 13(2), pp. 94-101.

Crielaard, J.M. and F. Pirnay, "Anaerobic and Aerobic Power of Top Athletes", European Journal of Applied Physiology, 1981; 47, pp. 295-300.

Fink, W.J., D.L. Costill, and M.L. Pollock, "Submaximal and Maximal Working Capacity of Elite Distance Runners. Part II. Muscle Fiber Composition and Enzyme Activities", Annals of the New York Academy of Sciences, 1977; 301, pp. 323-27.

Housh, T.J., W.G. Thorland, G.D. Tharp, G.O. Johnson and C.J. Cisar, "Isokinetic Leg Flexion and Extension Strength of Elite Adolescent Female Track and Field Athletes", Res. Quarterly for Exercise and Sport, 1984; 35(4), pp. 347-50.

Karikosk, O., "Training Methods for the 800 Meters" in Middle Distance Running, Tafnews Press, 1985.

Kindermann, W. and J. Keul, "Lactate Acidosis with Different Forms of Sports Activities", Can. Journal of Applied Sports Sciences, 1977; 2, pp. 177-82.

Komi, P.V., H. Rusko, J. Vos and V. Vihko, "Anaerobic Performance Capacity in Athletes", Acta Physiologica Scandinavia, 1977; 100, pp. 107-114.

Krusmann, R. and P. Schmidt, "Stepping Up To 800 Meters", Track Technique, Winter, 1985; 91, pp. 2900-2901, 2911.

McArdle, W.D., G.F. Foglia and A.T. Patti, "Telemetered Cardiac Response to Selected Running Events", Journal of Applied Physiology, Oct., 1967; 23(1), pp. 566-70.

McKenzie, D.C., W.S. Parkhouse and W.E. Hearst, "Anaerobic Performance Characteristics of Elite Canadian 800 Meter Runners", Canadian Journal of Applied Sports Sciences, 1982; 7(3), pp. 158-60.

Nurmekivi, A, "Training Methods in Middle Distance Running" in Middle Distance Running, Tafnews Press, 1985.

Pollock, M.L., A.S. Jackson and R.R. Pate, "Discriminant Analysis of Physiological Differences Between Good and Elite Distance Runners", Research Quarterly for Exercise and Sport, 1980; 51(3), pp. 521-32.

Popov, Y. and A. Zhurbina, "Strength Preparation of Women Middle Distance Runners", Soviet Sports Review, Mr., 1979; 14(1), pp. 6-7.

Rusko, H., M. Havu and E. Karvinen, "Aerobic Performance Capacity in Athletes", European Journal of Applied Physiology, 1978; 38, pp. 151-59.

Schnabel, A. and W. Kindermann, "Assessment of Anaerobic Capacity in Runners", European Journal of Applied Physiology, 1983; 52, pp. 42-46.

Scholich, M., "East German Study of the Distance Stride", Track Technique, Winter, 1978; 74, pp. 2355-59.

Svedenhag, J. and B. Sjodin, "Maximal and Submaximal Oxygen Uptakes and Blood Lactate Levels in Elite Male Middle and Long Distance Runners", International Journal of Sports Medicine, 1984; 5, pp. 255-61.

Svedenhag and Sjodin, "Physiological Characteristics of Elite Male Runners In and Off-Season", Canadian Journal of Applied Sports Sciences, 1975; 10(3), pp. 127-33.

Taunton, J.E., H. Maron and J.G. Wilkinson, "Anaerobic Performance in Middle and Long Distance Runners", Journal of Applied Sports Sciences, 1981; 6(3), pp. 109-13.

Thomas, T.R., C.J. Zebas, M.S. Bahrke, J. Araujo and G.L. Etheridge, "Physiological and Psychological Correlates of Success in Track and Field Athletes", British Journal of Sports Medicine, June, 1983; 17 (2), pp. 102-109

Verhoshansky, U. and V. Sirenko, "Strength Preparation of Middle Distance Runners", Soviet Sports Review, Dec. 1984; 19(4), pp. 185-90.

Withers, R.T., R.G.D. Roberts and G.J. Davies, "The Maximum Aerobic Power, Anaerobic Power and Body Composition of South Australian Male Representatives in Athletics, Basketball, Field Hockey and Soccer", Journal of Sports Medicine and Physical Fitness, 1977; 17; pp. 391-99.

Withers, R.T. and R.G.D. Roberts, "Physiological Profiles of Representative Women Softball, Hockey and Netball Players", Ergonomics, 1981; 24(8), pp. 583-91.

Wyndham, C.H., N.B. Strydom, A.J. VanRensburg and A.J.S. Benade, "Physiological Requirements for World Class Performance in Endurance Running", S. African Medical Journal, Aug. 1969; 19, pp. 996-1002.

THE ANAEROBIC THRESHOLD— FROM EUPHORIA TO CONFIDENCE CRISIS

by Manuel Bueno, Switzerland

A carefully documented summary of the controversial subject of the anaerobic threshold, looking at several aspects of the problems in its interpretation for the guidance of training.

INTRODUCTION

For about 20 years anaerobic threshold appears to have been the key parameter in the defining of the ability of a subject to maintain an exercise of sub-maximal intensity. In the past few years, however, the anaerobic threshold has become a controversial subject. The purpose of this article is to summarize the debate and, at the same time, to reassure the confused coach that "absolute" truths resulting from research have "relative" realities.

DEFINITION

The anaerobic threshold is defined as the power level of an exercise after which the energy needs of the organism can no longer be covered exclusively by aerobic metabolism. Also, as the critical power beyond which a steady state of lactate can no longer be maintained.

Expressed in percentages of VO_2 max the anaerobic threshold is unique for each individual and can vary considerably between the subjects with the same VO_2 max. It also happens that the margin to improve the anaerobic threshold is much larger than that for VO_2 max, even if these two variables are not entirely independent (di Prampero 1987).

TECHNIQUES

The anaerobic threshold concept remains a complex problem today and numerous proposals exist to determine the critical power of an exercise that provokes the break in the linearity of certain physiological or biological variables during an incremental exercise. The most often used are the following:

- **ventilatory** method (Fig. 1, curves 1 and 2), which uses the respiratory parameters (Wasserman 1964)
- **lactate** method (curve 4) (German school)
- **Conconi** method, which uses the heart rate (Conconi 1982) (Curve 3).

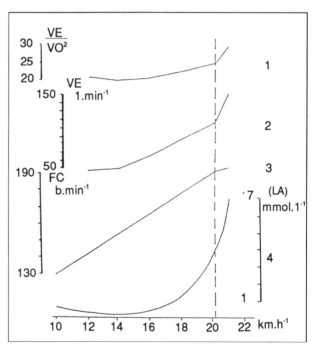

Figure 1: The curves of lactate (LA), heart rate (FC), ventilatory debit (VE) and respiratory equivalent of the oxygen (E. Jousselin 1986)

If the anaerobic threshold concepts were entirely clear, the deviation points of the variables should coincide (as in the ideal example in Fig. 1). However, this is not the case in reality, as divergencies between the results of various thresholds exist and the authors frequently contradict themselves. The

German school, for example, offers several methods according to whether the critical power is defined by:

- a fixed value of lactate equal to 4 mmol/l (Mader 1976)
- a fixed deviation point on the lactate-power curve in which the tangent is equal to 51° (Keul 1979) or to 45° (Simon 1981)
- a point on this curve determined by the total lactate kinetics, because, contrary to the previous cases, lactate is analyzed in the recovery phase after the exercise. As this point varies in the subjects, it is known as "the individual threshold" method (Stegman 1981) (Fig. 2).

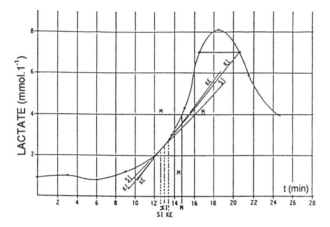

Figure 2: Determination of the threshold according to various methods: M—Mader (3 mmol/l); KE—Keul (tangent to 51); SI—Simon (tangent to 45); KI—Kindermann-Stegmann (individual) (Hedtkamp 1984)

DIFFICULTIES

In the ventilatory method the spirometric parameters fail to give information that allows us to predict athletic performance, nor does it aid in planning a training program. As for the other methods, the simplest is the Conconi test, although it is not as precise as the controversial lactate methods.

The estimation of running speed derived from the fixed threshold level of 4 mmol/l also has shortcomings. It appears to have an inherent weakness in not allowing the attainment of a steady state situation in the lactate metabolism (Stegman 1982). Thus, anaerobic thresholds can be found at considerably different lactic acid levels (Kindermann 1984, Hedkamp 1984, Simon 1984, Marti 1985).

There are problems related to the methodology. A laboratory analysis of the performance requires a precise, specific method of measurement and the

ergometer should be adapted, as much as possible, to the athlete's specialty (treadmill for runners). The nature of the exercise has an influence on the test results: the threshold lowers when the exercise is performed on a cycle ergometer compared to the treadmill. Moreover, the diversity of the protocols used and the variability of the results obtained increase the confusion. When incremental exercises test with 3 to 4 minute stages, the lactate-power curve varies according to the duration of the stages and recovery phases (Heck 1985). Add to that the lack of standardization of the testing equipment, the difficulty in transferring treadmill speeds to training speeds and so on, and the reliability of these tests becomes questionable.

An exact estimation of the organism's total lactate and its kinetics is extremely difficult. The complexity of all the phenomena is revealed by the differences in the lactate concentration observed in the muscles, in the venous blood and in the arterial blood (Yoshida 1982, Rieu 1986, Duvallet 1987).

A particularly interesting point is presented by the alterations in the intra-muscular concentrations of glycogen. After a low carbohydrate diet or a hypoglycemic state (fatigue, overtraining) the disassociation between the ventilatory and lactate thresholds can be accentuated and the shape of the lactate curve (also the Conconi curve) can deviate to the right. This signal, often interpreted as an improvement of the performance capacity, actually could indicate that there is a risk of overestimation of the real capacities of the subject. (Busse 1986, Braumann 1987, Lehnertz 1988).

The blood lactate concentration depends not only on the intensity of the exercise but also on its duration. The same concentration after 30 seconds does not have the same significance as a concentration that occurs after 10 minutes. Further, it does not indicate what happened during that time (di Prampero 1986).

This leads us to such basic problems as the relationship between blood lactate and anaerobics, which is not necessarily as close as previously suggested, the distribution of lactate between muscle cells and the extracellular environment, and even the significance of the blood lactate concentration that, in fact, only represents an instanteaneous balance between lactate production and removal during an exercise with a constant load (Brooks 1985, Rieu 1986, Rusko 1986).

The biochemical aspects linked to lactate metabolism are very complex and the phenomena in the current state of knowledge are very difficult to judge (Poortmans 1986). Too many uncertainties still exist to affirm several points.

CURRENT TENDENCIES

Recent literature abounds in recommendations for the use of the individual threshold, which offers a greater reliability in the diagnosis of performance and permits the introduction of more certain training structures. (Stegmann 1981, Marti 1985). The adoption of the 4 mmol/l threshold can lead, according to the same authors, to a false evaluation of the aerobic capacity of the subject. Fig. 3 illustrates the results of a double prolonged exercise test performed with the same group of subjects but with different intensities. One group used intensities that corresponded to their individual thresholds, the other group 4 mmol/l. In the case of the first group the exercise was maintained for 50 minutes without difficulties. The second group, on the other hand had to be stopped due to inability to maintain a steady-state blood lactate concentration (Stegmann 1982).

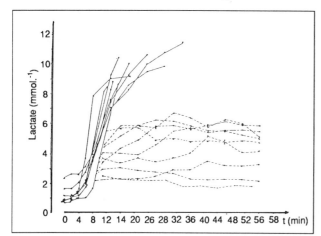

Figure 3: Test performance of 7 rowers
Cont. line = 4 mmol/l threshold
Broken line = Individual threshold (Stegmann 1982)

It is an absolute must that laboratory tests are accompanied by field tests. The last are more specific and provide more precise information for the planning of training, although there are difficulties with reproduction and standardization. Contrary to the laboratory tests, the constant in the field tests is the distance (about 2000m). The time, which diminishes progressively from one repetition to the other, is the variable (Schwaberger 1984, Fohrenbach 1984, Szogy 1986, Schmidt 1984, Jakob 1988). A particularly useful field test for performance diagnosis and the planning of training is the "two-speed test" (Mader 1980).

LACTATE STEADY-STATE

So far we have referred mainly to laboratory

tests with progressive loading in 3 to 4 minute stages. In these tests the "transitory" effects accumulate and the data applicable to endurance performance appears to be questionable. Currently a number of authors prefer the "stationary state" approach that looks for the maximum power output in which a steady-state of the blood lactate concentration can be maintained (Pinto Riberio 1986, di Prampero 1986, Antonini 1987).

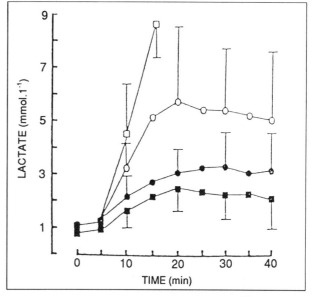

Figure 4: Lactate measurements at 4 different exercise levels (Pinto Riberio 1986)

Certain authors place the critical level at the anaerobic threshold level, others around 70 to 80% of the VO_2 max (Rieu 1986, Antonini 1987). There also are extreme variations between the steady-state blood lactate concentrations, ranging from 1.8 to 6.1 mmol/l (Stegmann 1982). Even 10 mmol/l has been mentioned (di Prampero 1987).

Considering that lactate kinetics are difficult to interpret, the concept of a maximum lactate steady-state as an indicator of the subject's aerobic capacity cannot be proved (Rieu 1986).

CONCONI METHOD

The determination of the respiratory threshold requires a spirometer, the lactate threshold a biochemical laboratory. All that is complicated and expensive. The Conconi method represents a simple alternative. However, it may only appear to be simple, as many wrong evaluations can occur if the test is not conducted precisely. The test also requires a sufficient number of reference points, especially in the area where the deviation occurs.

The Conconi method has its critics (Pinto Riberio

1985, Jakob 1986, Leger 1987, Kindermann 1987, Uhrhaussen 1988). The main reproaches are the lack of reliability, the nonexistence of the deviation point and the difficulty in the regulation of the progressively increased speed. This author resolved the last problem by using a commercial pocket computer that is carried by the athlete and is programmed to produce bips in the required rhythm. Beacons, placed every 25m around the track, provided the reference points.

COLLABORATION

The analysis of physiological test results and their application as a guide to establish optimal training intensities requires a close collaboration between the doctor and the coach. This dialogue is possible only if the doctor is competent in the problems of training and the coach has a solid knowledge of exercise physiology. In this doctor-coach-athlete relationship each has a role to play. And let us not forget that, besides the scientific and technical knowledge, there are simple things like the coach's intuition and the athlete's feelings that should never be underestimated.

DISCUSSION

Perhaps the most attractive aspect of the threshold is its correlation with the performance level in endurance events. The correlation becomes higher as the distance increases (marathon in particular). However, all the disputes have over the last few years produced a lack of interest among the coaches and athletes.

The methodological difficulties mentioned above, the incorrect test interpretations and the poor diagnoses have undoubtedly contributed in various degrees to this climate of insecurity (Busse 1987).

It is therefore necessary to admit that the threshold concept is not irrefutable. Too many uncertainties still exist to give the concept physiological significance (Rieu 1986). Even if precautions are taken, there are several sources of possible errors along the chain of operations, implicated by the processes employed (Lehnertz 1988). Consequently, endurance training can take place under "false intensities." If they happen to be too high, there is the risk of "burning out." Further,

by using the lactate method the threshold can differ by as much as 2 mmol/l (Fig. 2) (Hetkamp 1984, Simon 1985, Heck 1985).

There remains the possibility of using the Conconi method. It is within the comprehension of any coach who is well aware of the techniques and follows the protocol. It is necessary to avoid, as much as possible, irregularity in the heart rate—speed line, a serious problem in windy conditions. The Conconi test appears to be particularly valuable for running events, provided it is well executed. Nevertheless, the Conconi method is still criticized on the scientific level. The reasons for the behavior of the heart rate at the deviation point are not clear, nor is the relationship between this heart rate and the anaerobic metabolism (Ceretelli 1986).

CONCLUSION

It was not the intent of this author to put the anaerobic threshold on trial but to emphasize the difficulties and limitations that exist. The threshold concept is not a dogma and consequently we must accept its results not as an obligation but rather as a direction. The notion of the threshold, by whatever methods are chosen to determine it, is important to evaluate the work capacity of an athlete for a prolonged exercise, provided strict standards are applied to test procedures. If interpreted and repeated under regular medical guidance, the threshold can provide a practical parameter for the planning of training, particularly when it is accompanied by field tests.

I would like to conclude with a statement of great importance. We must not forget that the application of the threshold concept remains exclusively limited to the quality or the intensity of endurance training. In no way can it inform us on the optimum quantity or work load an athlete can tolerate. The last fact is closely related to fatigue and regeneration after intense physical loads, a problem abundantly discussed in current literature.

It is the direction that research is headed in the biological domain. This is of great importance, as the training of distance runners today employs virtually the same methods everywhere and it is not the most trained athlete that succeeds but he who recovers the best.

THE CONCONI TEST

by Hanspeter Probst, Switzerland

The anaerobic threshold is an important parameter in the guidance of middle distance running training. It was usually determined by blood lactate levels in complicated laboratory procedures until the Conconi Test was introduced. Although the accuracy of the Conconi Test has been questioned by some sport scientists, it nevertheless has been accepted as a reasonably reliable and simple field test.

INTRODUCTION

In 1982 Professor Conconi presented to the World Congress of Sports Medicine a relatively simple field test to ascertain the anaerobic threshold of runners.

The test was based on the fact that the heart rate (HR) increases linearly in a load range of approximately 120-170/minute. The increase moderates when the HR climbs over 170-180/minute. For a better understanding of this behavior, it is necessary to have some knowledge of performance physiology.

The cardiovascular system is responsible for the delivery of the required oxygen to the muscles in the aerobic work range. An increase in the work load leads to more energy needs and the oxygen consumption increases. This additional work is reflected in an increased HR. In the anaerobic work range the oxygen requirement of the muscles exceeds the supply in the blood. If the load is increased further, the additionally required energy must be produced locally without oxygen. The increases of the blood supply to the muscles, and with it the HR, are now limited. This metabolism produces lactic acid.

CONDUCT

The athlete, after a 15-20 minute warm up, runs on a 400m track a 200m section in a predetermined initial time and reduces the time by 2 seconds in each of the following 200m sections. The HR and the running time are recorded after each 200m.

The athlete therefore increases the running speed after the first 200m and continues to do so after each following 200m section until unable to increase it further.

Distance

The start for the first 200m takes place at the finishing line of the 100m on a 400m track. This allows the athlete to keep an even pace on the back straight before the 200m values are recorded. We use poles or bags to mark the 200m distances.

Data Collection

A pulse measuring device is needed to record the HR of an athlete during the run. To stop and count the pulse would lead to lower HR rates and ruin the test. A good device is the Sport Tester PE 3000 of Polar Electro, Finland.

Two methods are used to ascertain running speed:

    a) without a pacer;
    b) with a pacer.

Data Collection Without a Pacer
Initial Time

The choice of the initial time depends on the training condition of an athlete. The load should be selected so that the HR is within the 120-130/minute range. This corresponds to an initial time of 70 seconds for poorly trained "athletes" and 60 seconds for endurance trained athletes.

Running Time

The basic formula requires that the running time is reduced after each section by 2-3 seconds. Timing takes place with a split mode stopwatch (for example, Heuer 1035). This way the first 200m time can be displayed to check that the athlete actually has reduced the running time as desired.

The following practical procedures have proved to be helpful:

The athlete starts at point 1 where an assistant

also is present. When point 2 is reached, the athlete reads the HR from a pulse measuring device, notes it, and immediately steps up the pace. The assistant notes the 200m split. At the return to point 1, the athlete calls out the noted HR, as well as the now displayed HR, to the assistant, who in turn times the second 200m and records the information, etc.

The calling out of the HR's assures us that they have been correcty taken, a reason why we prefer this method to the use of a sport tester with a storage capacity.

Approximately 12-16 measurements take place in keeping up with the recommended reductions of the running time. This means that the athlete runs in approximately 10-12 minutes a distance of about 2400-3200m.

One of the best middle distance runners of the 80s, Brazil's Joaquim Cruz, shown here in an 800m victory over Sebastian Coe in Cologne in 1985.

It is possible to conduct two tests at the same time. In this case the second athlete starts from point 2. Testing more than two athletes together is not recommended, as they will only interfere with each other.

The recording sheet should contain, besides the name, place and date, the athlete's age, because the behavior of the HR is strongly influenced by it.

Data Collection With a Pacer

The following four difficulties occur when the test is conducted according to the above described method:

- The athlete selects a wrong initial speed (usually too fast)
- The athlete fails to keep constant speed over the 200m sections
- The speed is not correctly increased after each 200m
- The athlete accelerates too fast during the transfer to anaerobic work.

To overcome these shortcomings, we have developed the following system:

Both 200m distances are marked in 10m sections. A small computer produces peeping signals. The pace is correct when the athlete is close to a marker at the time of the signal. The frequency of the signals is increased after each 200m section.

Timing is now made unnecessary as the running speed has already been set.

We select 11 km/h initial speed for athletes with poor endurance and 12 km/h for well trained athletes. The speed is increased by 1 km/h after each 200m.

ANALYSIS

Analysis Without a Pacer

The split times (sec/200m) have to be converted after the track test into km/h. The formula is:

$$v = 720/t \text{ (t = split time)}$$

This is followed by the establishment of a graph of the HR and km/h values, in which the points of this pair are taken from the recording sheet. After all points have been transferred to the graph, an attempt is made to find a breakaway point from the linear. The quality of the test is revealed here. If the test procedures have been chosen correctly, the deflection point is easy to find.

The identification of the deviation needs a little practice. It is helpful to keep in mind that it can be found around an HR of 210 minus the age.

Conconi defines the HR at this point as pd and the speed as vd (see Figure 1).

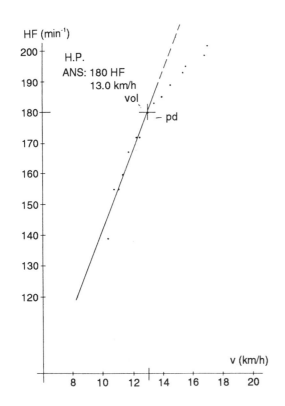

Figure 1: Determination of the Anaerobic Threshold (Conconi)

Analysis With a Pacer

No conversion of split times is required. The HR speed graph can be established directly. The analysis is made even simpler when an interface and a compatible IBM computer are available. There are computer programs on the market (HRCT Leuenberg Medicine Technique AG), that make an automatic analysis of the test possible.

APPLICATION

Training Condition

We discovered the following values in our tests:

Fitness Category	vd
Poor	10.0
Sufficient	12.0
Excellent	14.0

The values for junior distance runners at the end of the season ranged between 15.5-17.7 km/h.

As the heart rate depends strongly on the age, quoting pd and p max has no value. As a rule, the formula for the max for poorly trained men is HR pd max = 200 - 0.6 x age, for women 195 - 0.7 x age (pd is approximately 10 heart beats lower).

It is important to understand that the anaerobic threshold indicates only aerobic performance ability and not aerobic capacity. In other words, a single test tells me how fast the athlete can run without lactate production, but not how long the athlete can race at this speed. A so-called supertest is needed to find an answer to this question (see below).

Training Recommendations

Training recommendations should be made only in the aerobic range, because there is a close relationship between HR and the workload in this range.

Endurance runs are usually divided into four categories. According to experience it is possible to give rough guidance to the training intensities and durations, in which the vd, taken as 100%, is as follows:

ENDURANCE RUN

Category	Intensity %	Duration (min.)
Long	75	90-120
Slow	80	50-90
Medium	90	30-50
Fast	95	20-50

The choice of the intensity and its training frequency depends on the activity, training period and the actual form of an athlete. It must be decided by the coach.

It is possible to roughly evaluate the anaerobic capacity of an athlete on the results of the 200m sections covered in the anaerobic range.

Training Effect

The test can be repeated after approximately one month under the same conditions. A shift of the curve to the right (vd had increased) indicates an improvement of endurance ability, a shift to the left (vd has reduced), a deterioration.

SUPERTEST

A supertest is used to ascertain the aerobic capacity. Several Conconi Tests are conducted on the same day one after another. Similar results in the different tests indicate good long duration endurance.

BIOMECHANICAL RELATIONSHIPS IN DISTANCE RUNNING

by Keith R. Williams, Ph.D., USA

A detailed description of a number of relationships involving biomechanical aspects of running which are derived from the research by the author and others.

The following is a summary of information derived from quantitative research studies of elite and well-trained distance runners. It does *not* summarize the current state of knowledge resulting from a stastistical analysis of research data. Instead, it is a description of relationships involving biomechanical aspects of running which are derived from distance running research by the author and others over the last twelve years. All of the relationships suggested have a quantitative basis, but some elements of intuition and logic have been mixed in. Some of the relationships may be shown to be incorrect or in need of modification in the future, but they should provide some general guidelines for application to distance runners. None of the suggestions should be taken to be globally applying to all runners, because there are numerous individual exceptions. The intent is not to explore the topics in detail, as each could merit a lengthy discussion, but merely to introduce some of the concepts that might be of interest to coaches and runners. Many of the relationships will be nothing new to coaches, but they all do have some conceptual basis based on research findings. Comments, criticisms, and other insights or suggestions are welcomed by the author.

RELATIONSHIPS WITH OVERUSE INJURIES

Impact Related Injuries: There are a number of runners who have markedly higher than average ground reaction forces during the time the foot is in contact with the ground. These athletes are probably at more risk of developing injuries related to loading stress such as stress fractures, plantar fasciitis, shin splints, etc. Often there are no easily recognizable features of their running mechanics that would indicate that they run with high forces. In general we have found that forefoot and midfoot strikers tend to have slightly higher forces on average than do rearfoot strikers, though there are numerous individual exceptions. Particularly susceptible to these types of injuries seem to be middle distance runners who land in the forefoot. Interval training in shoes with little or no shock absorption may increase loads on the lower extremity to levels that lead to greater injury susceptibility. It is also likely that there are features of lower extremity structure and/or running style that predispose a runner to high forces and greater injury risk. The best way to prevent impact related injuries is probably to use sound judgment while increasing training intensity and to use good footwear. Runners who do have high impact force levels or a history of impact related problems should use shoes with good shock absorption characteristics.

Pronation Related Injuries: Overpronation has received a lot of attention from coaches, runners, clinicians, and footwear manufacturers. There are a large number of individuals who have injuries related to overpronation, such as chondromalacia, other knee pain, plantar fasciitis, etc., but there are also individuals who overpronate who have never had any problems. Overpronation may increase the likelihood of injury, but it does not guarantee that injury will occur. Limited pronation can also be a problem. A moderate amount of pronation is beneficial to the runner because it aids in shock absorption. With limited pronation other tissues (or shoes) must take over some of the shock attenuation needs, and this may lead to other stress related injuries. Many of the problems associated with over- or under-pronation are due to structural anomalies in the foot and lower leg. Flat feet often show greater pronation (though not always), and rigid high-arched feet often pronate very little. A history of pronation related injuries might help identify

52

individuals with such problems, as could biomechanical testing or clinical examination. Extremes can often be identified visually by carefully watching the running movements from the rear. Individuals with pronation related problems can often be helped by appropriately prescribed (by orthopedists or podiatrists) orthotics or by using footwear with effective rearfoot control properties. Overpronators want a shoe with features that effectively control motion, while those with limited pronation would not want such features and instead should get a shoe with good shock absorption capabilities. Overpronation is sometimes caused by crossing the foot over a midline of the run. When the foot lands across a midline the foot must pronate more in order to get flat. Running with a slightly wider foot strike pattern will reduce the amount of pronation and might relieve some symptoms in a runner who crosses over excessively.

Muscle Strains: While muscle strains are usually caused by doing more "work" than the body can safely withstand, there are probably musculoskeletal features that interact with errors in training causing a strain. Poor flexibility is likely to increase the chance of muscle strains, and muscle imbalances might cause an individual to work at an intensity that stresses the weaker side. Often there are limitations to movements or asymmetries in running mechanics caused by flexibility problems or muscle imbalances. For example, limited hamstring flexibility can lead to less flexion at the hip during running and result in lower than usual knee lift. Or weaker hamstrings on one side of the body might cause less extension on that side and lead to uneven stresses in the hip region. When movements are limited by flexibility constraints, muscles and other tissues must take on loads that they may not be prepared for. Particular attention should be taken when returning to running after a layoff due to an injury.

Mechanism of Injury: Overuse injuries occur when the body is subjected to repeated levels of stress that are greater than the body can sustain. A hard workout breaks down various tissues at the microscopic level and the body responds by building stronger tissue if given adequate time to do so. Knowing the appropriate time needed is the difficult part. If degradation occurs at a rate faster than the body can rebuild, an overuse injury may result. Training too hard too soon can result in injury, whether it be at the beginning of the season when the runner is not in good shape, or at the end of the season when at peak fitness. The challenge for the coach is to be able to perceive how to balance intensity and rest for a given athlete.

RELATIONSHIPS WITH PERFORMANCE

At this time I would say there are no features of running mechanics that can be said to be the trademark of the top level performers. Elite runners show a diversity of running styles that is as great as is found in lower level competitors. No one running style seems to be best in relation to performance. The style that is best for a runner is probably dictated by functional and structural characteristics. Strength, flexibility, size, joint structure, muscle characteristics, and many other factors all interact to influence which style is best for a given runner. At the same time there are numerous mechanical principles that should not be violated by runners. For example, running with vertical oscillation above a certain level is detrimental to performance because of the work that must be done against gravity. A coach with a runner showing excessive vertical movements should probably work at reducing them, but that does not mean that the lower the vertical oscillation, the better. At some point the benefits from lowered vertical movements are countered by adverse limitations to other movements. Thus, while some general features of good mechanics might be identified and used for guidelines, specific application to an individual must also take into account many other factors.

RELATIONSHIPS WITH FOOTWEAR

Oxygen Consumption: There can be small, but potentially significant, differences in energy costs during running in different types of shoes. The mechanism of such benefits is not understood well at present, but it is likely to be related to altering the patterns of muscular activity in such a way that less oxygen is needed. This would likely involve changes in movement patterns of the body segments, but such changes have not been explicitly identified as yet.

Typically the differences in energy costs are not greater than 1-2%, though that can be a meaningful difference to the runner. For example, lower energy costs have been associated with lower shoe weight and with good cushioning properties. Running shoes today have a multitude of features that may influence metabolic energy costs, and it is very difficult to assess how a given shoe will interact without extensive testing. Lightweight racing shoes are likely to have associated lower energy costs, but such benefits must be balanced against the probable increased risks due to running in shoes with typically less shock absorption and motion control.

Ground Reaction Forces: The shock absorbing capabilities of shoes can be influenced by both the design and materials used in construction. Air, EVA, and polyurethane materials can all be equally effective when appropriate design criteria are used. Differences in ground reaction forces can be seen between types of shoes. While these differences are typically small, in the range of 1-5%, they may be important to the runner. A lack of quantitative data concerning the properties of commercially available shoes makes it difficult to objectively identify how a shoe will influence force levels. The consumers are usually left basing their choices on qualitative information, anecdotal experiences, or advertising claims.

Motion Control Features: The design and materials used in shoe construction can influence the ability of the shoe to control movement in the rearfoot and forefoot. Again, a lack of quantitative information makes it difficult to associate specific shoes with certain properties. Differences between shoes are typically not large, in the range of 1-2 degrees, but even these small differences may alter stress distribution in the lower extremity in a beneficial (or detrimental) manner. Features such as rigid heel counters, external counters, firm material under the medial side of the shoe, and other similar features do seem to contribute to better motion control. Equally important is how well the shoe fits the runner's foot, and runners should try several brands.

RELATIONSHIPS WITH FOOT AND LOWER LEG STRUCTURE

Foot Structure: As previously mentioned, features of running style such as pronation are influenced by foot structure. A rough assessment of flat vs. normal vs. high arched feet can be obtained by looking at a barefoot print. Assessing whether the foot is flexible or rigid is more difficult and usually it is wise to involve a clinician if previous injury history indicates possible structural influences on injury. Bowed legs will increase the amount of pronation that occurs and may also alter stresses at the knee and hip. Knock-knees can also affect knee stresses and often influence the movement patterns of the legs, particularly during and following toe-off. Knowledge of structural features of the lower extremity can often help to identify why a runner moves in a particular way and might suggest changes that might be made to relieve stress to the tissues.

Leg Length Differences: Substantial differences in leg length (for discussion purposes, say greater than 1 centimeter) occur in a limited number of runners. Most do not have any associated problems, which probably means they have adapted to the difference through some structural or functional means. For example, sometimes the long leg shows greater pronation than does the short leg, and the increased pronation serves to effectively "shorten" the longer leg. It is usually not easy to see any influence on running mechanics due to a short leg. Since only one leg is in contact with the ground at a time, the other leg may not "know" that it is shorter or longer. Walking would be a different situation since both legs are on the ground at times, and the body may have adapted to this in a manner which would affect running. When there are associated problems, a heel lift will often help, though a very small height should be initially introduced with gradual increments over a period of time to allow the body time to adapt to the altered stress distributions. Orthotics are another, more expensive, option. A runner with a leg length difference but no related problems may develop some over a period of years as training intensity is increased or other injuries alter stress levels within the body.

Foot Length: Differences in foot length are not common but also not extremely unusual. While there is not a direct influence on mechanics, care should be taken to fit the longer foot to a shoe and use an insert to take up space in the roomier shoe.

Orthotic Devices: Prescription orthotic devices obtained from an orthopedist or podiatrist make the difference of being able to run or not being able to run for many runners. They are cast to conform to the foot and include supporting material on the undersurface of the orthotic that re-orients the foot into a mechanically more sound position, ideally relieving stresses that may have led to injuries. Often the differences in pronation associated with the use of orthotics are very small (a half degree to one degree), but the changes to stress levels must be sufficiently large since many runners have been helped by them. Orthotics will not help every runner who has lower extremity problems, and they are expensive, but they can provide relief not obtainable through any other means.

RELATIONSHIPS WITH OXYGEN CONSUMPTION

Individual Differences: There is good evidence that running mechanics can influence energy consumption during running. Unfortunately, there do not appear to be many relationships that can be applied to the majority of individuals. Rather, there is likely to be a set of mechanical features that is optimal for a given individual, and those features will be different from the ones optimal for another individual. Some of the general indications are identified below. A goal should be to work on fine tuning the mechanics of a given runner in relation to that runner's body size, structure, strength, flexibility and muscle characteristics rather than trying to make all runners fit an idealized model.

Kinematics: To date, weak to moderate correlations have been found between measures of body movements (kinematics) and oxygen consumption. There is some indication that lower metabolic costs are associated with greater extension of the lower extremity during the toe-off phase. There is also some evidence associating rearfoot landing patterns with lower energy costs, though many individual exceptions are found. At faster speeds of running these relationships may not apply since few runners continue to land on the rear of the foot. Though there is not strong supporting scientific evidence at this time, it is logical that greater energy cost would be associated with runners with excessive vertical oscillation, or with runners who show large decreases in forward velocity following footstrike necessitating a similar magnitude increase during the push-off phase.

Stride Length: Studies have suggested that most runners will find their most efficient stride length through a self-optimization process. There will still be some runners who can lower energy costs by slight modifications to stride length. My perception is that most of these individuals are overstriding compared to understriding. Particularly susceptible might be shorter runners who run at stride lengths that are long relative to their leg length.

RELATIONSHIPS WITH FATIGUE

Changes in Kinematics: Some kinematic measures seem to change with speed. For example, stride length tends to lengthen, and runners usually flex the knee more during the swing phase as they get fatigued. What is unknown at this time is whether such changes are beneficial or detrimental. Is the change in movement patterns a consequence of not being able to maintain usual muscle activation patterns resulting in a less efficient style? Or do the altered movements actually make the body more efficient by involving muscles in a slightly different way and reducing the strain on fatiguing muscles?

Injury: The likelihood of injury is increased when running fatigued. Muscles often act to lessen the stress on other lower extremity tissues, and when they get fatigued and movement patterns change, tissues which usually do not sustain high loads must take on some of the burden. Thus a tissue which may be sufficiently strong under normal conditions may become the weak link when fatigue alters the distribution of stresses. This may be more of an issue for training than for racing. In racing, fatigue cannot be avoided since performance is the overriding consideration. However, during training it might be more rational to balance the physiological benefits of extreme levels of fatigue with the potential musculoskeletal risks. A cleverly devised training regimen might be able to achieve the same physiological benefits without causing intense localized muscle fatigue that puts the runner at greater risk for musculoskeletal injuries.

EVALUATION OF PERFORMANCE INDICATORS IN MIDDLE DISTANCE RUNNING

by V. Kulakov, N. Kromtsov, USSR

The authors present a graded testing system, based on aerobic, anaerobic, speed and strength indicators, to evaluate the preparation level of middle distance athletes.

What are the most important factors that decide the specific physical preparation of middle distance runners? The basic factors are the aerobic and anaerobic work capacities, speed qualities and strength potential.

AEROBIC CAPACITY

The aerobic work capacity is the dominating factor in performance. The most important indicators of this are maximum oxygen consumption, the critical running speed and the speed at the anaerobic threshold. The speed at the anaerobic threshold is the most useful of these indicators for practical use (the running speed of an athlete is determined at a lactate level of 4 mmol/l, interpreted as the speed at the anaerobic threshold). Under normal situations this indicator is based on the results of a 3 x 2000m running test in which the speed is increased in each of the three phases (blood is taken after each phase).

The speed at the anaerobic threshold can also be determined by using pulse indicators that record the heart rate and the time of the running phase. The test is based on continuous running on a measured track with a step-by-step increased running speed (Conconi test). The time of each part distance (200 to 1000m) and the heart rate are recorded and transferred to a graph. The deviation point on the graph indicates the speed that corresponds to the anaerobic threshold of the athlete.

What can be done when sport testers are not available?

The same procedures can be used:

The pulse rate is taken manually and transferred to the graph for the determination of the deviation point. However, it must be kept in mind that the pulse rate drops extremely fast after the run has been completed (45 in the first 15 seconds). It is therefore necessary to take the pulse within 10 seconds after the completion of a running phase. At least four phases should be incorporated in the test and the last phase must be covered at close to maximal effort. Most suitable for this test is the employment of 300m or 400m distances.

ANAEROBIC CAPACITY

The quantitative indicator of anaerobic work capacity is the athlete's work power in a performance of 1 to 2 minutes in duration and the maximal lactate concentration after this. That is the reason why we have chosen to test anaerobic work capacity with a 600m run, after which blood is taken every minute over a period of 4 to 5 minutes to determine lactate.

A pre-determined lactate concentration of HL=16 mmol/l can be used when the analysis of blood samples is not possible. This can be done by using the following formula:

$$K_{an} = 10^{-4} V_{av}^3 \times \sqrt{HL}, \text{ in which}$$

V_{av} = average running speed of the 600m distance (m/sec.).

HL = pre-determined lactate concentration 4 to 5 minutes after the 600m run (mmol/l).

OTHER INDICATORS

Speed qualities in a fatigued situation can be simply determined by using a test to establish the time needed to cover 200m. The test consists of a 200m sprint at maximal speed, conducted seven minutes after the completion of the 600m anaerobic capacity test.

The most informative *strength potential* quality indicators can be based on four basic tests:

1. Maximum number of pull-ups
2. Number of push-ups in the front lean position
3. Number of straight leg lifts over the head to the hands in hanging position
4. Number of one-leg squats.

A complex strength indicator can be calculated from the results of the four tests by using the following formula:

$$K_s = \frac{9P + 50 + 5L + 6S}{26}$$

K_s = complex strength
P = pull-ups
O = push-ups
L = leg lifts
S = one-leg squats

TOTAL FACTORS

All of the single indicators can be presented in a 10-point system to evaluate the specific physical performance factors of long distance runners (as shown in Table 1) and have great practical value in the evaluation of distance runners.

10 points in the table corresponds to ideal quality, 6 points to USSR master of sport model, 3 points to Class I model. However, because all the factors do not have equal value, the physical preparation level of a distance runner is best calculated according to the formula.

$$K \, phy. = \frac{4Ae + 3An + 25p + 1St}{10}, \text{ in which}$$

Ae = Aerobic qualities
An = Anaerobic qualities
Sp = Speed qualities under fatigued conditions
St = Strength qualities.

Table 1: Test indicators presented in a graded model.

Point system	Aerobic-speed at anaerobic threshold (min.)	Anaerobic (K_{an})	Speed qualities (200m result)	Strength potential (K_s)
10	below 2.52	over 2.0	below 22.0	42 and more
9	2.52-2.56	1.8-2.0	22.0-22.7	38-41
8	2.56-3.00	1.6-1.8	22.8-23.5	34-37
7	3.00-3.06	1.4-1.6	23.6-24.5	30-33
6	3.06-3.15	1.2-1.4	24.6-25.5	25-29
5	3.15-3.25	1.0-1.2	25.6-26.5	19-24
4	3.25-3.40	0.8-1.0	26.6-28.5	14-18
3	3.40-4.00	0.6-0.8	28.6-29.5	9-13
2	4.00-4.20	0.4-0.6	29.6-31.0	4-8
1	over 4.20	below 0.4	over 31.0	0-4

MEANS OF DEVELOPING SPECIFIC ENDURANCE IN MIDDLE DISTANCE RUNNING

by Phil Lundin, USA

Competition-specific training for middle and long distance runners can be accomplished in many ways. In the following article, Phil Lundin, Assistant Track Coach, University of Minnesota, discusses information on preparatory competitions, time trials and modeling with some specific examples.

The normal training scheme within athletics is founded upon the principle of progression. This principle refers to the development of general physical abilities during the preparatory period(s) with a gradual transition to training forms which enhance the main qualities inherent to the event during the competitive period(s) of the yearly training cycle. Generally, the competitive period differs from the preparatory period in reduced volume and increased intensity of workloads. This is accomplished by greater attention to the inclusion of training exercises which mimic the main competition-specific qualities of the event proper.

In the training of middle distance and long distance runners, the development of endurance is achieved in several phases: 1. general endurance; 2. the development of a foundation for specific endurance; 3. specific endurance (Bompa, 1983). General endurance is improved primarily through uniform, continuous runs of great duration at moderate intensities during the early preparatory period. The development of a foundation for specific endurance is achieved through a combination of uniform and alternative continuous runs with long and medium interval training during the preparatory period. Specific endurance is the primary objective of the pre-competitive and competitive periods with the following exercises generally used to accomplish the objective: 1. preparatory competitions; 2. time trials; 3. model training.

The above training scheme presents a plan similar to the "Lydiard method" whereby athletes use the various training means one after the other with very little mixture (Kruger, 1973). Such a format will place competition-specific exercises in the late preparatory and competitive periods only. The "complex method" of endurance training mixes the various training means throughout the yearly cycle, stressing different ones at different times. This type of plan will include competition-specific exercises throughout the year, although special emphasis upon such training will take place during the competition period(s). It must be kept in mind that the use and placement of such exercises in the yearly training cycle is a variable dependent upon the training philosophy and individual differences among endurance athletes. What will follow, then, is an investigation of the various means of enhancing competition-specific endurance.

PREPARATORY COMPETITIONS

Generally, athletes can contest only up to three or four main competitions a year. It is essential that such competitions should be approached in the order of difficulty leading systematically to the most important event of the year (Haare, 1982). Studies regarding means and techniques used in the long-term planning of training with regard to peaking indicate that 7-12 competitions are sufficient to reach a high state of readiness for major competitions (Bompa, 1983 & Haare, 1928). The frequency of preparatory competitions depends largely on the demands of the event, individual tolerance to training and the athlete's training age. Because endurance events place an extra demand on energy reserves, it is recommended that at least 7 to 14 days separate competitions. Younger athletes may compete more frequently but careful monitoring is essential to allow for recovery. Preparatory competitions at related distances to the competitive event are useful in the development of competition-specific qualities and allow some variety in the training preparations.

To aid in the systematic planning of the training cycle, Dick (1978) has described four categories of competitions of varying psychological and physiological intensities:

1 — simple training competitions — low intensity
2 — build-up competitions — progressive intensity
3 — main competitions — maximum intensity
4 — competition climaxes — maximum intensity

Competitions which require no effort are valueless. Also, the psychological load which accompanies the competitive experience increases dramatically as one progresses from simple training competitions to competition climaxes. This is the primary distinction between the various categories of competitions, for high to maximum efforts are necessary to all starts to evaluate the athlete's progress and to adapt to competitive stress.

TIME TRIALS

Time trials are a means of simulating a competition-specific environment and of assessing the fitness level of athletes. The use of time trials is included in many programs such as Lydiard's training schedules and the Oregon system (Doherty, 1985, Bowerman, 1974) In the above-mentioned systems, the time trials are planned so improvement continues evenly from trial to trial. Lydiard utilizes such exercises only in the track training phase (competitive period) of the yearly cycle, whereas the Oregon system includes time trials throughout the year. Both systems use sub-maximal intensities in such trials, not maximal efforts, with emphasis on achieving a pre-determined time at even pace. Such systems require careful and realistic goal setting and appropriate progressions in the use of the time trials.

In reference to time trials of maximal intensity, Yakimov (1982) states that careful consideration should be given to the frequent use of such exercises due to the negative effects on the athlete. Such a situation may be avoided by the substitution of preparatory competitions, or progressive, sub-maximal time trials incorporated into the yearly training cycle. If maximum intensity trials are incorporated into the training plan, distances should be chosen which exploit the same energy systems as the competitive event but are of $1/2$ to $3/4$ the competitive distance. Such exercises are also excellent means of developing pace judgment.

MODEL TRAINING

Modeling is the approximated reproduction of the basic peculiarities of a competitive activity in the process of training. It denotes a somewhat altered and approximate imitation in training of future competitions (Matveyev, 1981). Model training is used primarily during the competitive period because of its specificity. Microcycles (weekly training periods) may be "modeled" based on the specific requirements of a competition. Examples of a competition modeled week may be the alternation of high intensity or simulated competitive days with days of rest which mimic the competitive schedule of preliminary and final competitions. Training sessions falling on the same day as a competition in an upcoming contest should be very demanding while those falling on a day of no competition should be of lower intensity. Also, the daily training lessons should be taken at a time and within an environment as similar as possible to the upcoming competition.

Specific workouts may also be modeled. Yakimov (1981) states that it is difficult to simulate within training physical reactions which correspond precisely to those encountered in competition. Running the competitive distance at full effort may accomplish the necessary specificity, but as previously mentioned, the use of such exercises generally leads to negative effects on the athlete's spirits. Such a problem led to the development of the modeling method. The idea behind the method is to reach within the course of a workout a heart rate achieved in racing. At that time, a brief rest is given to allow a slight repayment of oxygen debt and a drop in heart rate not to exceed 15 beats/min., after which the athlete returns to the workout. This simulates racing conditions, yet does not wear an athlete down as much as time trials or competitions. The basic principles of model training according to Yakimov are:

- the rest should be fairly short—the heart rate should drop no more than 15 beats/minute
- the work interval should decrease in length
- the first interval should be equal to, or slightly shorter, than half the racing distance
- the total running time should be close to, or better, than the athlete's best time over the distance.

An example of model training used for an 800m runner with a personal record of 1:50:

1 — 400m race pace——55 seconds
2 — rest 20 seconds (or allow a drop in the heart rate of 15 beats/min.)
3 — 200m in 26 seconds

4 — rest 10 seconds or as in 2
5 — 200m in 28 seconds

Total time = 2:19
Total running time = 1:49

Another version of model training is offered by Bompa (1983) who defines modeling as a variation of repetition training with its originality due to its resemblance to the specifics of competition. The workout is divided into three parts. The training commences with several repetitions much shorter than racing distance at an intensity equal to, or greater than, race pace. Justification for this is offered in light of the fact that the anerobic system is tapped as is the case early in a race. The mid-portion of the workout consists of repetitions over distances which will improve and perfect aerobic endurance. In order to exactly model the race, the last part of the training sessions employs shorter repetitions at maximal effort to simulate the final kick. Such factors as total volume, velocity, rest intervals and number of repetitions have to be determined according to the athlete's potential and race characteristics. Bompa recommends using the heart rate method to calculate rest intervals. The following is an example of a 4:20 miler following the above guidelines:

1 — 2 x 400m 63-64 seconds
2 — rest, HR = 140 before resuming work
3 — 1-2 x 1000m 2:55—3:00
4 — rest, HR = 140
5 — 2-3 x 200m 30-31 sec. (100m recovery jog).

Another variation of model training are simulation drills as described by Dellinger (1984).

The simulation drills are designed to simulate the race by having the runner cover portions of the racing distance at "goal" pace, the other parts run at a slower pace to allow the completion of the entire racing distance. As the year progresses, the goal pace portions of the drills increase accordingly until the drills evolve into an exercise more akin to the modeling described previously. As noted, such simulation drills are progressive in nature and generally used throughout the yearly cycle up to and through the competitive period.

In summary, competition specific training for middle and long distance runners can be accomplished in many ways. General information and specific examples of preparatory competitions, time trials, and modeling have been discussed. The utilization of such methods must be adjusted by the coach to fit the needs of the athletes. It is essential that training of such high intensity is carefully incorporated into the training cycle with close monitoring of the athlete's adaptation and recovery.

REFERENCES

Bompa, T. (1983). *Theory and Methodology of Training*. Dubuque: Kendall/Hunt.
Bowerman, W. (1974). *Coaching Track and Field*. Boston: Houghton Mifflin Company.
Dellinger, B., & Freeman, B. (1984). *The Competitive Runner's Training Book*. New York: Macmillan Publishing Company.
Dick, F. (1978). *Training Theory*. London: British Amateur Athletic Board.
Doherty, K. (1985). *Track and Field Omnibook*. Los Altos: Tafnews Press.
Haare, D. (1982). *Principles of Sports Training*. Berlin: *Sportsverlag*.
Kruger, A. (1973). "Periodization, or Peaking at the Right Time." *Track Technique*, 54, pp. 1720-1724.
Matveyev,. L. (1981). *Fundamentals of Sports Training*. Moscow: Progress Publishers.
Yakimov, A. (1981). "Middle and Long Distance Training Methods." *Track Technique*, 83, pp. 2633-2637.

STEPPING A FEMALE 400m RUNNER UP TO THE 800m

by Tony Benson, Australia

Australian National Middle Distances Coach Tony Benson discusses the problems involved in stepping a women 400m exponent to the 800m, with some detailed advice on the organization of training in the early stages of the transition to the longer event.

Lothar Krieg in *Die Lehre der Leichtathletik* (Vol. 24, No. 31, 1985) suggests the main problem in changing from 400m to 800m centers around the need to improve the athlete's aerobic capacities substantially, while continuing to further develop anaerobic endurance. Tactical considerations and the strengthening of the willpower are further requirements for a successful transition, according to Krieg.

In this light he makes the following suggestions:

- Make the transition slow and gradual
- Aim for a high level of aerobic endurance
- Emphasize 600m in training and avoid overdistance work
- Use one or two 600m runs at 800m pace prior to competition to develop pace judgment
- Do not delay the change to 800m until later in an athlete's career
- Run only a few selected races in the first season
- Combine endurance training with tactical practice and
- Stress the need for a persistent attitude if some "failures" occur.

These recommendations form, in a general sense, an excellent basis for any coach to begin planning a 400m to 800m transition. Specifically, however, a number of key questions remain to be answered.

Over what period and at what intensity does "slow and gradual" refer to? How high is a "high level" of aerobic endurance and, even more importantly, which methods should be used to achieve this? What changes will need to be made to the 400m anaerobic endurance methods already being employed to make the training more specific to 800m? And with the extra workload and with less units of work being devoted to pure speed, how can

the coach attempt to maintain the athlete's 400m speed base?

Another aspect that the coach must keep in mind is the fact that, in general, the 400/800m type has been less successful at the international level than has the 800/1500m type, although this difference is not as pronounced among women as it is among men. It is also significant to note that, while the men's world record is held by an 800/1500m runner (Sebastian Coe), Jarmila Kratochvilova, a 400/800m type, holds the women's record. On the other hand, the quality of women's 400m and 1500m records suggests that, comparatively, the 800 meters should be at least 1:52.8 and perhaps as fast as 1:50.4 if it were to be of equal value to the 1500m or 400m respectively.

METHODS

The coach will be faced with two distinctly opposing approaches in attempting to implement the transition from 400m to 800m.

Method 1: Train the athlete to extend upward from 400m as the coaches of Alberto Juantorena and Jarmila Kratochvilova did, basing everything on maintaining, even improving 400m bests, while at the same time employing low volume, high intensity training to develop 800m speed endurance.

Method 2: Follow something like the Lydiard approach and increase the training volume dramatically while, especially in the conditioning phase, reducing the intensity equally dramatically.

The decision of which method to follow is very important because the 400m runner will probably need anything from three to six years to reap the benefits of the chosen method. If, after that time has elapsed, the choice is deemed to be less than satisfactory, there will be very little time to implement the other approach, unless the athlete was very young when the change of event was first decided upon. Hence the wisdom of Krieg's advice in not delaying the change of event for too long.

One aspect of this, however, is that it is far more likely that reverting to a speed approach from the aerobic base would be more successful than trying to move up from the anaerobic method to a long distance oriented one. There are both physiological and psychological reasons for believing this.

Physiologically it takes a number of years to develop a high level aerobic base and the athlete may arrive at the twilight of her career before the effects of the change begin to influence performance.

On the other hand, it would probably take only one or two seasons for an athlete to change successfully to a low-volume speed-oriented approach. Such a procedure closely parallels what occurs in a yearly cycle anyway, as the athlete moves from the buildup or preparation period to the competition period.

Psychologically, changing from the endurance approach to a speed one would also be easier. Under the speed regime the 400m runner will already have experienced some discomfort in accommodating the demands of 800m training such as running 500 to 1000m repetitions instead of the accustomed 150 to 300m runs. If now, on top of the perceived failure to achieve the 800m goals, the athlete is asked to increase the volume of both individual and unit training, as well as the time spent at training, he/she may well decide that it is simply not worth the effort and retire.

Alternatively, an athlete asked to reduce both the total volume and repetition/interval length could find the change an enjoyable challenge.

THE BUILDUP PERIOD

Based on the second method there are two aspects to the buildup. The first is to reach an acceptably high yearly volume, which seems to be between 1280 and 3200km for the experienced international athlete. The second is to decide what methods to use. There is a choice of low intensity continuous runs (pulse <130), moderate intensity continuous runs (pulse 130-150) and moderate to high intensity continuous runs (pulse 150-180). Next comes the question of how to disperse these throughout the major training phases and how to integrate the training units into an overall program which must also include the development of speed,

speed endurance, and power.

The obvious place to start is the yearly volume. Assuming the athlete should be reaching an optimal volume within three to four years of the change it becomes a simple mathematical matter to calculate the yearly increments needed to move from the athlete's present load up to the required volume.

Once the yearly total has been decided, the coach can move on to distributing that total through the various phases. My suggestion is to allocate 65 to 67% of the total volume to approximately 60% of the year which is devoted to either building up or rebuilding after a first peak. A further 21 to 25% could be allocated to the approximately 24% of the time devoted to the pre-competition period with the remaining 10 to 12% of volume being allocated to the competition phase.

During the buildup phase the coach could then plan the following units of training into the weekly plan:

- A relaxed session with tempo maintenance as the focus. Such a session would gradually become more speed specific as the year progresses but would always stay within the parameters of a 100-200m type of workout. As Peter Coe is quoted saying, "If speed is the goal, then never get too far from it." (The 1983 IAAF Symposium on Middle and Long Distance Events).

- A long run. This could begin as low as 6km and gradually build up to 10 to 12km for the 400/800m type and 15 to 18km for the athlete who shows an aptitude for 1500m as well. This run is definitely slow and easy the majority of the time.

- Two other easy days where the athlete's aim is recovery.

- One day devoted to gaining strength via any form of resistance running, such as hills, sand, running in weighted vests or harness work.

- A session designed specifically to increase aerobic fitness. This could be a fartlek workout away from the track, containing surges of 500 to 1000m, or from 1.30 to 3.30 minutes at 65 to 75% effort, followed by recovery periods of approximately the same time, to a steady to fast pace run through hills which allows the rise and fall of the terrain to dictate the effort and recovery rhythm.

- One anaerobic workout, using 100 to 400m distances, with recovery periods of 45 to 90 seconds and covering between 3 and 5 kilometers in total.

In terms of controlling the aerobic intensities, the

long run and the running that is done on the two easy days would, on most occasions, be in the low to moderate range. The session designed specifically to develop aerobic fitness would always operate in the moderate to high range. Further high intensity aerobic benefits would also be gained from the anaerobic-aerobic session.

THE PRE-COMPETITION PERIOD

This period can follow basically the same rhythm to include:

- One day aimed at the development of optimal 100-200m speed, although the session itself should be easy enough for a full recovery in less than 24 hours. Distances beyond 80m would be the exception rather than the rule.
- The long run as usual.
- The two easy recovery runs as usual.
- A more intensive unit of resistance running would be introduced.
- The anaerobic-aerobic session aimed at the 800m would be similar in structure to the one contained in the previous phase but slightly shorter and more intense. Sets and pyramids would also be introduced.
- A 400m specific session would replace the general aerobic workout of the buildup period.

THE COMPETITION PERIOD

This period is not as easy to outline in terms of a general structure because it contains a number of variables that have to be dealt with on a daily or weekly basis.

These include adjusting training in the light of strengths and weaknesses as revealed by the initial race, changes to the originally scheduled racing program and differentiating preparation workouts prior to major and minor races.

THE MAJOR RACE PREPARATION

Generally a 7 to 10 day plan is to be recommended. One example of such a plan might be:

DAY 1:   A normal 800m session.
DAY 2:   An easy recovery run of normal length.
DAY 3:   A 400m session or a sprint session.
DAY 4:   A long run (90 to 100% of the usual weekly run).
DAY 5:   An easy recovery run.
DAY 6:   A specific proven pre-race session.
DAY 7:   An easy recovery run of normal length.

DAY 8:   An easy day.
DAY 9:   An easy day.
DAY 10: THE RACE.

THE MINOR RACE PREPARATION

Follow the normal weekly program with perhaps a little more freshening up 3 to 4 days prior to the race.

This weekly program would not be significantly different from the training done during the pre-competition phase. Where differences might be apparent would be in the reduction of the overall volume, the emphasis on quality, the decrease of quantity, the increase of recovery times in the 400 and 800m sessions and the shortness and sharpness of the sprint workouts.

What is important to remember, however, is that the real work has already been done and that attempts to make further gains in terms of additional fitness are quite likely to be counter-productive. Concentration on recovery, rhythm, pace judgment and tactically oriented training track relaxation will produce much better results.

THE FIRST YEAR OF THE TRANSITION

The first year will really be crucial to the 400m runner's chances for future success in the 800m. It is important to keep in mind that, no matter how well the transitional process appears to have gone, the athlete is not yet an 800m runner. Therefore the number of races over 800m, especially for the less experienced athlete, must be limited to as few as four to six.

The results must be successful, which means that the coach must set conservative goals. Being conservative is an especially valuable coaching tool because the athlete will either achieve or exceed the set goals. Either way the stage has been set for a successful transition.

As important as restricting the number of races is controlling how the races will be run. Remember, this is an inexperienced athlete with a 400m background who is very likely to start far too fast. Tactical considerations have to be taken into account. A 400m runner is accustomed only to racing in lanes, so group training can be very instructive. This involves performing intervals and repetitions in a bunch, sprinting off the curve with four to six athletes initially confined to the first two lanes of the track and so on.

The development of an 800m rhythm is essential because the race is not an extension of the 400m in the same way as the 400 is of the 200m. For example, in running 47.6 for the 400m Marita Koch was able to sustain 91% of her 21.71 speed over 200m. On the other hand, Jarmila Kratochvilova was only able to sustain 84% of her 47.9 400m speed in her 800m time of 1:53.28. Repetition runs over 400 to 600m could be of value in this regard.

The coach also may have to alter certain aspects of the athlete's auxiliary program. The amount of running drills and starts would obviously be reduced; bounding and plyometrics, which do not combine well with increased weekly running volumes, might be better replaced with resistance running methods. Weight workouts will possibly need restructuring towards the trunk and upper body areas and circuit training could assume as much, if not more, importance as weight training.

Specific advice is very difficult to give in these areas because certain athletes and their coaches highly recommend some or all of the auxiliary methods, while others achieve the same success using none of them. No better example of the diversity of training regimes which have produced outstanding results can be cited than a comparison of Sebastian Coe's, Steve Ovett's and Steve Cram's approaches.

On the other hand, it must be kept in mind at all times when planning the program that, regardless of what methods are decided upon, the athlete has only a finite amount of time and energy to devote to training, so a careful balance must be maintained between what is introduced and what therefore has to be deleted.

A paradigmatic example of the 400m runner extending upward successfully to 800m, Czechoslovakia's Jarmila Kratochvilova, who set world records at both distances in the early 80's.

CHAPTER III

APPROACHES TO
TRAINING

MIDDLE DISTANCE RUNNING TRAINING METHODS

by Alfred Pisuke and Ants Nurmekivi, Estonia

A classification of middle distance running training methods according to energy supply processes with a short definition of four types of methods employed in a complex approach to training procedures.

INTRODUCTION

An efficient preparation of middle distance runners depends largely on a well-planned periodization of the training year, usually based on the following scheme:

1. The preparation period (November to May, 28 to 30 weeks), divided into four separate phases:

- An introductory phase (end of October to end of November)
- The first basic training phase (December-January)
- The winter competition phase (February)
- The second basic training phase (March-April-May).

2. The competition period (June to September, 16 weeks), divided into two separate phases:

- The first competition phase (end of May-June)
- The second competition phase (July to September)

3. The transition phase (October, 3 to 4 weeks).

In order to get the best results from a periodized year, training processes must incorporate the most suitable training methods to develop performance capacities. The methods employed by middle distance runners can be divided into basic and secondary methods. The basic methods cover running in all its variations, the secondary methods are made up of general conditioning, strength, power, coordination and suppleness exercises, as well as games, skiing, swimming, etc.

CLASSIFICATION

The different methods used in training are classified (according to the energy supply processes being used) into aerobic, aerobic-anaerobic (mixed) and anaerobic categories. Anaerobic work in turn is separated into glycolytic-anaerobic and lactic-anaerobic methods. It should be noted that this classification is somewhat arbitrary because it is in reality impossible to use only one energy source in running. One or another process will only be dominating. Nevertheless, classification according to the dominating energy processes allows the achievement of the necessary changes in the athlete's work capacity most efficiently.

Table 1: Criteria for the evaluation of running loads.

Training Parameters	Blood Lactate (mg%)	Pulse (beat/min.)	% of Oxygen consumption from max.	Pulse Recovery
1. Restoration runs	up to 27	up to 130	50	below 60
2. Aerobic runs (steady-state)	up to 36	up to 160	60-70	60-70
3. Mixed runs				
Tempo cross-county	up to 50	up to 170	80	70-80
Extensive interval	up to 80	up to 190	90-100	---
4. Anaerobic runs (glycolytic)	over 80	over 190	over 100	80-90

Note: Pulse recovery is based on the sum of three 10 second counts, taken from the end of the run as follows: 0-10 seconds, 30-40 seconds and 60-70 seconds.

An objective middle distance training plan is based on the intensity of energy consumption, taking into consideration the difference between maximum oxygen uptake capacity and the oxygen actually used, pulse frequency, lactate concentration, the dynamics of the pulse recovery, breathing intensity and other indicators (Table 1). It is wise not to overlook subjective indicators but to combine them with the objective information.

The basic criteria in the evaluation of the intensity of training in middle and long distance running are the anaerobic threshold and the critical speed. The anaerobic threshold is the running speed that is followed by a sudden accumulation of lactic acid. The critical speed is the running speed at which maximal oxygen consumption occurs. Consequently the anaerobic threshold divides work between the aerobic and mixed regimens, while the critical speed borders work between anaerobic and mixed regimens.

METHODS

Aerobic Methods
The running speeds in aerobic training methods are kept below the anaerobic threshold. Running occurs in what is known as the steady-state, where oxygen intake and consumption are balanced. The blood lactate concentration is around 27 to 36mg%, oxygen consumption 50 to 70% from the maximum and the pulse rate about 130 to 160 a minute. The aim of aerobic training is to gradually improve the steady-state running speed.

Steady-state runs, performed over different length distances, form the basic approach to the development of aerobic endurance by improving the working economy of the cardiovascular system and metabolism. Other aerobic type runs are recovery and restoration runs. Recovery runs, with a pulse rate below 130 a minute, are performed between repetitions in interval running and during a warm-up. Restoration runs are used after demanding races and extremely hard training sessions.

Mixed Regimens
The mixed aerobic-anaerobic training methods range in their intensity between the anaerobic threshold and the critical speed. The intensity decides how much the anaerobic processes will have to contribute to the total energy production. The lactate concentration can therefore range between 36 to 80mg%, oxygen consumption 70 to 100% from the maximum and the pulse rate beteween 160 to 190 a minute. The aim of the mixed aerobic-anaerobic

training is to develop aerobic power and capacity, as well as to stimulate the development of the steady-state speed. The following methods are commonly used:

- Fast pace endurance runs (tempo cross-country runs). The intensity is adjusted according to a particular training task. Our studies have indicated that an intensity around a pulse rate of 165 a minute is the most economical. A pace above that brought about a sudden drop in the percentage of oxygen consumption and an increase in ventilation
- Runs under difficult conditions (hills, deep snow, sand, etc.) to develop maximal aerobic power and strength endurance. The emphasis on a fast drive and relaxation to develop local muscular endurance without a large accumulation of lactic acid is of primary importance here
- Fartlek with emphasis on medium and long accelerations that fit into the range of the mixed training regimen. Intensive short accelerations in fartlek should be regarded as anaerobic training
- Extensive interval runs, dominated by repetitions of relatively long distances (600 to 3000m).

Anaerobic Methods
Anaerobic training methods exceed the critical speed. Lactate concentrations reach over 80mg% and the pulse rate is over 190 a minute. The main aim of anaerobic glycolytic training methods is the development of speed endurance but anaerobic-alactic methods are also helpful to improve speed and acceleration capacities. The following methods are commonly used:

- Intensive interval runs, dominated by medium distance (200 to 600m) and aiming to develop a specific race speed. Recoveries are shortened as the racing speed is achieved. Shorter distances are often covered at faster than racing speed
- Repetition runs, characterized by fast speed and relatively long recoveries. The length of the distances employed depends on the race distance and a concrete training task
- Intensive uphill runs, adjusted in length and the number of repetitions to develop glycolytic or creatine-phosphate mechanisms
- Sprints and interval sprints over short distances to develop the ability to change running rhythm and the capacity to accelerate
- Bounding and jumping exercises (multiple jumps, uphill bounding, jumps over hurdles,

depth jumps, jumping up the stairs, etc.) for the development of leg power.

Although the volume of anaerobic methods is rather small in a year's training program, the value of these methods should not be underestimated.

MAJOR CATEGORIES

Besides a physiological classification, training in distance running can be divided into four basic categories as follows:

- The continuous method
- The repetition method
- The variable method
- The interval method.

It was stated at the Duisburg conference that contemporary training should be based on a combination of all the above-mentioned methods, distributed according to the demands of the different phases in the training year. As there have been conflicting and contradictory views on both characteristics of these methods, it appears advisable to explain them shortly.

Continuous Method

This method is employed by middle distance runners to develop general endurance and by long distance runners for event specific, as well as general endurance. It is the basic method in the preparation period but continues into the competition phase, where it is adjusted according to the demands of the racing distance.

The training load in the continuous method is usually determined by the mileage and running speed (intensity). However, it can also be determined by time (for example, running steadily for 90 mintues). The training load in this method is gradually increased in the initial stages, followed by either increasing the volume or intensity, or by leaving the volume unchanged and increasing only the intensity.

The continuous method, accepted as the basic training method during the preparation period, develops the cardiovascular system and improves ventilation and metabolism. It is particularly efficient to increase capillarization.

Repetition Method

Under the repetition method we understand the repetitive running of a distance with optimal recoveries. The duration of recoveries depends on the running speed and the length of the distance, ranging from 4 to 6 minutes (short distances) to 15 to 20 minutes. Short and medium distances are usually covered close to the average racing speed.

The repetition method is employed to develop speed, speed endurance and specific endurance.

Variable Method

This method, in contrast to the interval method, is not controlled by a strict pace, intensity and recoveries. It is usually employed to develop general endurance, event specific endurance, movement economy and occasionally also tactics. The variable method is also frequently used in the transfer from continuous running to more intensive work.

The load and intensity in the variable method is determined by time or mileage, sometimes also by the number and length of predetermined accelerations. The intensity is changed frequently and the chosen terrain should preferably have a variable profile. A common format of this method is fartlek (speed play), established by Swedish coach Gosta Holmer and employed mostly in the second half of the preparation period.

A typical example of fartlek could be based on the following:

- Easy running for 5 to 10 minutes
- Steady, relatively faster running over 1 to 2 km
- Easy variable running (accelerations within 50 to 60m until slight fatigue)
- Full speed uphill runs over 150 to 200m
- Relatively fast pace running for one minute, following the uphill runs.

Interval Method

The interval method is based on repetitions of a certain distance, or combination of distances, with insufficient recoveries, in which the length of the distance, the running speed and the duration of recoveries are predetermined. The interval method is usually divided into intensive (relatively fast) and extensive (relatively slower) workouts. It is employed mainly to develop event specific endurance.

The length of the distance varies between 50 and 3000m and can be used as repetitions of the same distance (for example 10 x 400m) or a combination of distances (for example, 100 + 200 + 300 + 400m, or 5 x 200m + 5 x 400m, etc.). Several authorities favor combinations to avoid monotony, others recommend the opposite. However, most agree that there should not be drastic differences in the length of the distances in one training session.

The running speed depends on several factors but, as a rule, shorter distances are covered at the

Table 2: Allowances to the average racing speed (seconds).

Training Distance	Men Women	Month							
		Nov.	Dec.	Jan.	Feb.	Mar.	Apr.	May	June
100m	M	1.6	1.4	1.2	1.0	0.8	0.6	0.4	0.2
	W	2.4	2.1	1.8	1.5	1.2	0.9	0.6	0.3
200m	M	4.0	3.5	3.0	2.5	2.0	1.5	1.0	0.5
	W	6.4	5.6	4.8	4.0	3.2	2.4	1.6	0.8
400m	M	8.0	7.0	6.0	5.0	4.0	3.0	2.0	1.0
	W	12.0	10.5	9.0	7.5	6.0	4.5	3.0	1.5
1000m	M	20.0	17.5	15.0	12.5	10.0	7.5	5.0	2.5
	W	40.0	35.0	30.0	25.0	20.0	15.0	10.0	5.0
2000m	M	40.0	35.0	30.0	25.0	20.0	15.0	10.0	5.0

average racing speed, or slightly faster, relatively longer distances at racing speed or slightly slower. An average speed calculation table (Table 2), based on expected average racing speeds is widely used. The table allows the establishment progression by making allowance for the training speeds prior to the competition season.

The recoveries in the interval method are predetermined, using a time limit (for example, 2 minutes), a set distance (for example, 200m jog) or a heart rate (for example 130 beats a minute). It is normally recommended that recoveries be shortened to develop anaerobic processes through creating an oxygen debt. This can be based by simply reducing the recovery times to start the next repetition with a higher pulse rate.

Volkov, for example, recommends distances from 200 to 600m at the maximum speed for the corresponding training period with the reduction of recovery intervals from 5 to 6 minutes to 3 to 4 minutes and finally to 2 to 3 minutes. This type of training should take place, combined with other methods, during the competition season.

The number of repetitions in the interval method varies considerably in individual training programs and depends largely on the training period and on the aim of developing general or specific endurance. The recommended yearly volume in interval training is summed up in Table 3.

Table 3: Yearly interval training volumes for middle distance runners.

Distance	Men (m)	Women (m)
400m	1600-2000	800-1600
800m	2400-3200	1600-3000
1500m	3000-4500	2400-4000

SUMMARY

The above-listed methods cover the basic approach commonly used in the training of middle distance runners. It is important to understand the good and bad sides of each of these methods because there is no universal approach to distance running training. Each training method has its own specific influence and different methods must be varied and combined for best results. It can be said that training should be based on a complex method but the complexity must be individual.

PRACTICAL REMARKS ON MIDDLE DISTANCE RUNNING TRAINING

by Dieter Petscha, Germany

A detailed discussion of the main factors in middle distance running training, including the planning of training, periodization, training methods and their place in a year's program.

THE PLANNING OF TRAINING

Considerations

- What do I want to achieve? What are the basic motor qualities (speed, strength, endurance) that need considerable improvement? (training targets)
- What emphasis should be placed on the development of certain motor qualities? (periodization of training)
- How are these motor capacities rated in view of an optimal distance specific performance? (loading norms)
- Which training methods and means are particularly suitable for this purpose? (training methods)
- What is the number of training units set for individual athletes? (training frequency).

The training units, according to Letzelter, are the smallest links in the construction of a training plan. They are identical to training days when training takes place once a day. What follows will be based on six training units a week and this obviously forces the inclusion in the program of the so-called mixed training units. It simply isn't possible in middle distance running to develop all general physical capacities separately in six days.

Mixed training units have shortcomings, as well as advantages. For example, it would be senseless to conduct sprint or strength training after an 8km tempo endurance run. On the other hand, training means to develop speed endurance have a good training effect in fatigued conditions after an aerobic load. Training means to develop sprinting speed can be included in a complex training unit to counteract stagnation created by endurance runs. However, it is important that sprint training, like technique development, takes place in rested conditions.

Central Concepts

According to Letzelter, H. and Letzelter, M. (1986) there are three central concepts applied to the planning of training:

1. Targets—the improvement of such capacities as speed, strength and endurance have priority in the targets of middle distance running. They are called motor training targets. However, also cognizant training targets must be taken into consideration to develop the movement quality, as well as effective training targets for hard training and racing. The last is particularly helpful to improve the willpower of the athletes.

2. Content—the content of training is always adjusted to meet the demands of the training targets and can therefore contain a lot of variety. This allows plenty of room for creativity in the choice of training means. The term of training means, according to Berhard (1972), "includes all means and measures that give the training processes organizational, informative and movement morphological support."

3. Methods—for explanation: A training target in middle distance running, for example, could be the development of speed endurance. In this case the contents of training could be 200 to 400m tempo runs and the training methods intensive interval running.

Other training targets in middle distance running besides the development of speed endurance, are:

a) the improvement of sprinting speed (basic speed)
b) the improvement of maximal strength, particularly in the muscles involved in the running action (movement speed)
c) the optimization of strength endurance and development of intra-muscular coordination
d) the improvement of running endurance.

The corresponding contents of training are:

a) short sprints (about 75m) with full effort in rested conditions, various starts, coordination exercises
b) weight training with sub-maximal up to maximal resistances with limited repetitions and series. Exercise intensity within the 70 to 90% range from the maximal performance
c) exercises that correspond closely to the running action with light or medium resistances and a large number of repetitions (bounding and jumping exercises with light weights, high knee lift runs, etc.)
d) endurance runs, fartlek, tempo runs.

The corresponding training methods are:

a) intensive interval method, repetition method
b) repetition method, intensive interval method
c) the main task in strength endurance training is to find the largest possible load volume that requires higher resistance than that in racing. Extensive interval method
d) endurance method, extensive interval method.

The training targets, content and methods and their correlation are summed up in Table 1.

According to Matveyev (1981) there is:

1. A phase during which the sporting form is developed.
2. A phase of the stabilization of the sporting form with a climax performance.
3. A phase during which the sporting form is reduced.

These criteria are transferred to a training year with the decision to opt for a single or a double periodized year. In addition, it is important to decide whether indoor championships are going to be treated as part of training or as the first performance climax.

The following text will look at the most common organization of a training year in middle distance running, divided into the transition, preparation (general and specific) and competition periods for a single periodization. A single periodization doesn't rule out a regeneration phase with an increased volume and reduced intensity. Performance lows

TABLE 1: A summary of the relationships between training tasks, content and methods.

TASK	STRENGTH	SPEED	ENDURANCE
CONTENT	a) Strength endurance b) Maximal strength	a) Sprinting speed b) Speed endurance	a) Aerobic endurance b) Anaerobic endurance
	To a): Running and jumping exercises with light and medium loads. Weight training on the same principle. High reps	To a): Full speed sprints up to distances around 75m	To a): Longer medium pace endurance runs, low intensity tempo runs
	To b): Weight training with sub-maximal and maximal loads. Low reps	To b): High intensity tempo and repetition runs	To b): Varied speed tempo runs, fartlek, high pace endurance runs
METHODS	To a): Extensive interval method	To a): Repetition method, intensive interval method	To a): Endurance method with a constant, partly variable intensity. Extensive interval method.
	To b): Repitition method	To b): Repetition method, intensive interval method	To b): As in a) but with a higher intensity

TABLE 2: A summary of training tasks in the single phases of a training year.

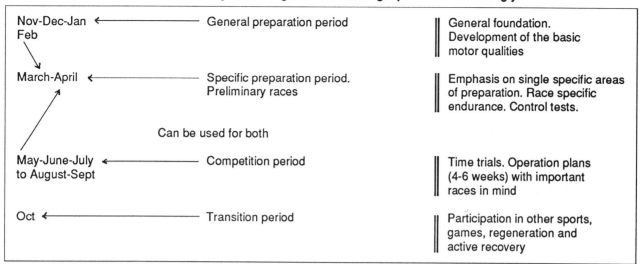

Nov-Dec-Jan Feb	← General preparation period	‖ General foundation. Development of the basic motor qualities
March-April	← Specific preparation period. Preliminary races	‖ Emphasis on single specific areas of preparation. Race specific endurance. Control tests.
	Can be used for both	
May-June-July to August-Sept	← Competition period	‖ Time trials. Operation plans (4-6 weeks) with important races in mind
Oct	← Transition period	‖ Participation in other sports, games, regeneration and active recovery

should be planned, as it is impossible for an athlete to maintain top form over a long time. Table 2 attempts to present the organization of the single phase in a training year.

The month of May counts as the preparation phase for higher performance level middle distance runners. However, for a large number of athletes facing district championships in June, the month of May belongs in the competition period.

The coach or the athlete usually plans for one training year. In contrast to a multi-year plan this means fixing less long-term targets and concentrating on short-term aims. According to Letzelter the deciding principles here are:

- To begin the new training cycle based on evaluation of race performances, race observations, motor tests and the previously conducted training
- To be guided by the analytically proven load dynamics, as well as the total load of the previous year or half-year
- To consider the relationship between general and specific, as well as conditioning and technical development in the previous cycle
- To structure the new cycle as single or double periodized.

TRAINING METHODS

The organization of the training methods and tasks in the different training periods have been presented in Figure 1. It can be added that long, steady endurance runs are in the foreground during November-December. Emphasis shifts to varied speed tempo runs, shorter and faster runs or long

runs with fast sections in February-March. Hill running is included at the same time (aim: to develop leg strength). Intensive interval training and repetition runs are emphasized during the specific preparation and competition periods. An early application of these training means leads to an early peak form and also to a following drop in the performance.

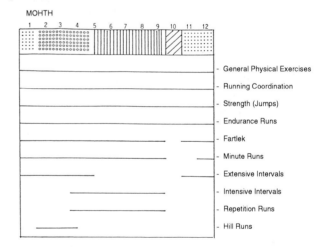

MOHTH

- General Physical Exercises
- Running Coordination
- Strength (Jumps)
- Endurance Runs
- Fartlek
- Minute Runs
- Extensive Intervals
- Intensive Intervals
- Repetition Runs
- Hill Runs

Figure 1: The Organization Of Training Methods

The following should be taken into consideration in the performance of endurance runs:

- An average pace of under five minutes per kilometer must be maintained even by juniors (male) in order to benefit from the physiological stimulus of the endurance runs
- The development of a "careless endurance run stride" must be avoided. It is advisable after longer endurance runs to perform two or three accelerations to break through the steady

contraction rhythm that developed in the working muscles during the endurance run
- It is not necessary for young athletes to begin with the development of aerobic endurance too early. The improvement of speed and general strength should be in the foreground because endurance can be effectively developed later.

Aerobic endurance running, because it improves considerably the oxygen uptake of the active tissue, has a positive training effect in middle distance running. As a result the athlete can run a long time in the aerobic range during a race. An athlete with a low aerobic capacity on the other hand, is forced to use anaerobic energy sources far too early. This, as the distance increases, reduces the performance reserves more and more. Athletes with a good endurance training background exploit their anaerobic performance potential much later in the race.

In addition, the highly endurance trained athletes have created a solid base for the following anaerobic training processes. This means that they have a better performance perspective, provided, of course, that speed training has taken place parallel to the development of endurance. However, one problem remains that many athletes simply don't have the time for the relatively high training volume.

SAMPLE TRAINING CONTENT

Cross-Country Running

General Preparation Period:

- Steady endurance runs, up to 20km every three to four weeks
- Runs over a wide variety of terrains
- Runs with higher intensity on flat terrain.

Specific Preparation Period:

- Endurance runs with higher intensity
- Once a week 6 to 8km with really high intensity
- Fartlek
- Varied speed tempo runs
- Hill running

Competition Period:

- Regeneration runs to escape from the track
- Hill running prior to races for the development of high stride frequency and relaxed action.

Track Running
General Preparation Period:

- About 6 x 1000m at a speed corresponding from 60 to 70% of the personal best. Recoveries five minutes or according to pulse
- About 8 x 600m at race speed corresponding to best 1500m time plus 15 seconds
- Minute runs (regressive pyramid: a) 4-7-9-6-5 minute (recoveries according to pulse); b) 2-4-5-7-6-3-1 minute (recoveries according to pulse; c) 1-2-1-2-1-2-1-2 minute (recoveries according to pulse); d) 3-4-5-4-3 minute (recoveries: previous load time minus 1 minute); e) 1-3-2-4-2-3-1 minute (recoveries equal to previous load time).
- 10 x 400m in 80 to 90 seconds
- 3 x 1600m in which the first run is at a steady pace; the other two with alternating fast and slow 100m
- 10 minutes endurance run with two 30 to 60 second fast tempo lifts.

The aim of all these training means is to develop aerobic endurance.

Specific Preparation Period:

- 3200m with a 50m sprint each lap
- 2000 to 3000m with an acceleration on each back straight and a 30m sprint each lap
- 2000 to 3000m with a 13 to 16 second 100m sprint each lap
- 200-300-400-300-200m with 200m jog recoveries
- 4-10 x 400m at 90 to 100% of the planned average 800m race speed. Recoveries 2-6 minutes
- 3-6 x 800m at 85 to 95% of the planned average race speed. Recoveries 3-6 minutes.

Competition Period:

- Series of tempo runs. For example, 2 x 3 x 300m in 10 to 12 seconds faster than best 400m time
- Pyramid tempo runs. For example, 300-400-500-400-300m. (300m 12 seconds faster than best 400m time, 400m 10 seconds slower than best 400m time)
- Tempo runs followed immediately with 50 to 100m high knee lift run, bounding or sprinting
- Runs with a predetermined time with some parts covered faster, others slower than the average pace
- 2-3 repetition runs at close to race speed covering under or over distances with full recoveries
- 4-5 repetitions of striding over 150m (two days before a race).

EXPERIENCES IN THE TRAINING OF 800 METER RUNNERS

by Olav Karikosk, Estonia, USSR

The author discusses his coaching experiences in the training of 800m runners, outlines his own early studies and those conducted recently in Germany. He comes to the conclusion that emphasis in the training of 800m runners should be placed on the development of the athlete's dominating performance qualities and individually suitable methods lead to the top.

PERSONAL EXPERIENCES

Once I got involved in coaching some talented distance runners, it became obvious to me that there were shortcomings in my knowledge and coaching ability. I discovered that my learning at the university had to be supplemented in the fields of physiology, as well as psychology. I also noted many conflicting and controversial aspects in the training programs of the world's best distance runners. It confused me until I realized that a systematic gathering and analysis of information can help to solve some of the problems and allows me to reach more objective conclusions than simply depending on the advice of certain authorities.

In 1962, I was astonished by the world 800m record of 1:44.3 by Peter Snell, who cut 1.4 seconds off the previous mark by Roger Moens. Surprising was not only Snell's actual time but also the information about the training methods he employed to achieve it. Snell, guided by Arthur Lydiard, exceeded during the preparation period the volume of many long distance runners (600 to 650km a month). Compared with the previous best 800m runners, Harbig, Whitfield, Courtney, Kerr and others, Snell's training volume was three times higher. Did all the other athletes employ wrong training methods, or were they using methods that suited them best?

At this stage I was coaching one of my best 800m runners, Rein Tolp, using the traditional training methods. Tolp's total volume was only 1713 in his best year but Lydiard's influence made me raise it considerably. It reached 3700km a few years later; however, not only did his times fail to improve, they actually began to slow down.

In an effort to find a solution to this problem I began to gather information on the training conducted by the world's and Soviet Union's best 800m runners. The collected data allowed me to divide the runners into three groups:

1. Athletes who have been particularly strong in the 400m but modest in the 1500m.
2. Athletes who have achieved reasonably good performances in both the 400m and 1500m.
3. Athletes whose strength is in endurance and frequently use the 1500m as their second event.

An analysis of the material led to the conclusion that relatively fast training runs with a limited number of repetitions and long recoveries were best suited for the first of the three groups. The nervous system and muscular structure of this group obviously allows them to tolerate fast anaerobic work in training. At the same time, however, their muscular and central nervous systems, influenced by uneconomical metabolism, become quickly fatigued. Consequently an increased training volume brings to this group negative results.

The second group of runners train with a somewhat reduced intensity but with shorter recoveries and a considerably larger volume. The metabolism of the athletes in this group is more economical and the energy reserves are larger. This delays the onset of fatigue in comparison to the first group.

The training pace of the athletes in the third group is generally the slowest but the volume considerably larger. Their metabolism is particularly economical, energy reserves are large and the cardiovascular system adapts readily to continuous training loads.

STUDY RESULTS

The results of the study convinced me that emphasis in training should be placed on the dominating performance qualities of an athlete. In general, it appears that a smaller volume of intensive training is suitable for the faster type of 800m runners, while a large volume of somewhat less intensive training benefits the endurance types. At the same time, however, the development of the weaker performance qualities should never be overlooked.

According to my own study, I should at this stage have continued to use the previous method of a gradually increased training volume. This, however, was not simple when an athlete belonged to the national team of the Soviet Union and everybody had to follow national training policies. In these days it was clear-cut—all 800m runners had to employ the methods of the current world record holder (Peter Snell).

As it turned out, Tolp, after being dropped from the Soviet team a little later, changed his approach to training and reduced the volume to 2800km a year. A year later he took the USSR title in Tsahkador, situated 2000m above sea level. It was an excellent performance, considering that he could not prepare for the race at high altitude training camps.

Once my studies had been published in *Legkaya Atletika* and translations appeared in several other countries, the Finnish journal *Jouksija* forwarded the information to Lydiard for comments. His comments appeared a little later under the title of "A Letter from Arthur" and were critical about my theory.

Lydiard claimed that "Karikosk suggests several ways to reach the top. This is not true because extensive aerobic training must always precede anaerobic work. There are many who wrongly believe that athletes can train several months anaerobically and improve their performances. George Kerr, who reached 45.8 seconds in the 400m, "killed" himself with his speed and interval training. Had he paid more attention to the development of endurance, he would have almost certainly been the gold medal winner in Rome."

There is no doubt that Lydiard was correct in claiming that aerobic training forms the base for anaerobic work. However, it should be kept in mind that the 800m is an event where anaerobic energy production is considerably larger than aerobic. The world record holders who followed Snell, Marcello Fiasconaro (1:43.7 in 1973) and Alberto Juantorena (1:43.44 in 1977), had training volumes three times smaller than Snell's. Both employed anaerobic training in their programs already in the preparation period. The present world record holder, Sebastian Coe, begins anaerobic work during the winter and his 350 to 400km a month training volume is smaller than Snell's.

No wonder *Jouksija* published in 1978 an article by British coach Frank Horwill with a statement that Jordan (USA), Karikosk (USSR), Nett (Germany), Letzelter (Germany) and Wilson (Britain) consider the importance of individual qualities in the training of 400m runners. Only Lydiard is convinced that everybody should use Snell's approach. This was followed by a 139 page study by Thomas Jeggle on 800m training in 1985, stating that my initial work, developed further by Edmond van den Eynde, is still viable.

THE VIEWS OF JEGGLE

Jeggle's piece included 17 top West German 800m runners and was based on an 11 page questionnaire and physiological tests. The last established aerobic and anaerobic capacities, including the anaerobic threshold, the volume of aerobic training and its quality, as well as the methods employed in anaerobic training. Based on this information Jeggle divided the runners into the following three groups:

1. The 400m type of middle distance runners who are mainly tall and have an athletic build. Fast twitch muscle fibers are dominant in this group. Their speed and anaerobic endurance capacities are large but the aerobic endurance capacity rather modest. Emphasis in training is mainly on the development of speed and anaerobic endurance.

    The maximum weekly training volume doesn't exceed 60km and cross country runs are limited to 8 to 13km. Repetition of short distances, seldom over 600m, make up most of the training, with the development of speed receiving particular attention. Circuit training, bounding and running exercises are used to develop power and strength endurance. Three runners, with a best time of 1:46.04, made up this group.

2. The 400-1000m type of middle distance runners, who also command a good anaerobic capacity. Their adaptation to aerobic work is better than the first group's (the 400m type). The weekly training volume is usually around 60 to 80km and makes use of series of repetitions of different distances with short recoveries. A lot of emphasis is again placed on the development of

Marcello Fiasconaro, seen here leading Josef Plachy in the 1973 Italy-Czechoslovakia dual meet. Fiasconaro set an 800m World Record of 1:43.7 in this race.

speed and power. The best athletes in this group included P. Braun (1:44.59). Assmann's weekly training volume was around 60km. He had good aerobic, as well as anaerobic capacities, and placed great emphasis on the development of speed and coordination. Speed, strength and endurance training were often combined in a training session.

Wulbeck's training was also dominated by quality but he was not involved in specific sprint training, adjusting most of his work around the race tempo. The weekly training volume was 90 to 100km, employing series of varied distances. Recoveries were short. Strength training was virtually absent in Wulbeck's program.

3. The 800-1500m type of middle distance runners, who command excellent aerobic capacity, but have relatively modest anaerobic endurance. Their emphasis in training is placed on the development of aerobic endurance, which also forms a base for the improvement of anaerobic endurance. The volume of training reaches up to 120km a week.

Athletes in this group often employ training longer distances at a pace considerably slower than racing speed. Specific endurance is developed by using various shorter distances with short recoveries. Sprint training is not effective for this type of 800m runner. Strength development takes place mainly by uphill runs.

IN SUMMARY

Looking at the different types of top-class 800m runners over the last two decades will help to clarify the outlined training theories. The information, including best 400, 800 and 1500m per-formances and the monthly training volumes during the preparation period, are presented in Table 1.

Table 1

Juantorena	44.26	1:43.44	3:45.5	170
Fiasconaro	45.5	1:43.7	--	190
Susanj	45.9	1:44.1	--	180
Ferner	46.97	1:44.93	3:46.0	320
Assmann	47.0	1:44.59	--	250
Coe	46.82	1:41.73	3:29.71	400
Cruz	46.0	1:41.77	3:36.4	400
van Damm	46.4	1:43.86	3:36.26	400
Wulbeck	47.83	1:43.65	3:33.74	400
Wohlhuter	48.2	1:43.4	3:36.4	500
Wottle	49.9	1:44.3	3:36.2	500
Ovett	47.5	1:44.10	3:30.77	550

In summary it can be said that the above mentioned studies and practical experience has confirmed that there is a firm correlation between the prerequisites and the training methods of 800m runners. All the different types of athletes can achieve world-class performances by using indivi-dually suitable training with emphasis on the development of their dominating performance capacities. My own experience has shown here that a systematic gathering of information can be extreme-ly helpful in solving many training problems.

TRAINING FOR MIDDLE DISTANCE

by Adam Zajac and Gregory Prus, Poland

An excellent overview of the most current thinking regarding the planning and organization of training for middle distances. The authors directly address the dilemma facing today's middle distance runner: a large number of races distributed over a long period of time. They present clear solutions to that problem, solutions which fit within the context of an overall training plan.

In recent years, the theory of track and field training has been faced with the following problems:

1. Preparing the peak of the athletic form for the right time;
2. Using the proper proportions of training methods in different phases of the yearly cycle;
3. Finding optimal training loads for individual athletes as well as arranging the proper sequence of training emphasis in the mezo and microcycles.

These problems have been further complicated by 2-3 daily training sessions. Ergogenic aids have also stimulated athletic performance and thus athletic training has reached an even greater range of interest.

Today some of these problems have been cleared up, yet new ones have developed. For most events in track and field, there are now two competitive seasons, yet for the distance runners the competitions last the entire year. Cross country and road races in the fall, indoor races in the winter, and the very long outdoor season which lasts from early spring to late summer.

If athletes are to compete the entire year the concepts of annual training cycles must change. Most athletes are not prepared to train at high volumes and intensities throughout the year. Too much volume causes stagnation. Overtraining can result quickly if intensity is abused in training.

Graph 1 presents a comparison of the traditional macrocycle structure, which prepares the athlete for 2-3 peak performances, and the new structure which is more elastic and allows for high performances throughout the year. The new time structures have identified phases of training which were not considered previously.

There are three major phases in the training process: Accumulation, Intensification and Transformation.

Phase I—Accumulation: This period of time is used to regenerate from previous competitions and to accumulate energy for the more intense training which will bring about the adaptive changes. Low intensity, high volume training is carried out in this phase. Variety of training is also very important for psychological recuperation.

Phase II—Intensification: The role of this phase is to elevate the aerobic and anaerobic endurance and increase the psychological resistance to stress induced by training.

Phase III—Transformation: In the third phase, the performed work should be transferred into effective athletic racing form.

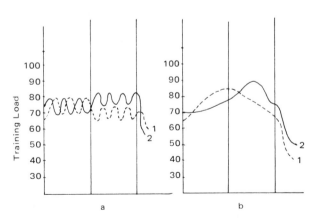

Graph 1: The dynamics of volume and intensity in the macrocycle. 1=volume; 2-intensity; a-new structure; b=traditional structure.

Table 1: Description of training stimulus.

Stimulus	Load	Forms of Training		Volume in Points
		Middle Distances	Long Distances	
Recuperation	indirect effect	Jogging CR_2	CR_1, CR_2	1
Maintenance	indirect effect	CR_2 circuit training	CR_3, Fartlek	2
Elevation	direct effect	Ext. Int. Fartlek	Ext. int., Tempo	2
High increment	direct effect	Tempo Int int.	Int int.	3
Races	direct effect	400-3000m	3000m-marathon	3

For example, a miler should perform the following type of workouts in the three consecutive phases:

Phase I—Extensive intervals: 16-20 x 400 in 75 seconds with 90-second rest period interspersed by days of LSD (15-20 km) or other sports.

Phase II—Intensive intervals: 8-10 x 400 in 58-60 seconds with 3- to 4-minute rest periods, interspersed with easy continuous runs over shorter distances (8-10 km).

Phase III—3-4 test races divided by active rest. We have assumed that an athlete preparing for a 1500 should run 2-3 control races at 800 and 1 or 2 at 3000m.

According to many experts the three phases should be included in every micro and mezocycle—A + 1 + T. There is no doubt that all the races have to be planned carefully into the macrocycle and that each of them should be preceded with a mezocycle constructed with the A + 1 + T phases.

The **DCP—Direct Competition Preparation** mezocycles are used by most middle and distance runners in Europe with great success. The traditional periodization approach had to be changed due to the increased number of competitions annually.

Many athletes compete 9-10 months a year. Maintaining a high level of performance throughout that span of time requires a very specific form of preparation. DCP mezocycles seem to be the best answer. Their structure is very logical and efficient.

The three phases which compose the DCP guarantee proper balance between volume and intensity, between work and rest. This time structure also creates the most suitable conditions for adaptive changes at the cellular level.

Most often the DCP lasts for 4-6 weeks, although it can be structured in different ways. Following are three examples of DCP mezocycles composed of six microcycles.

A. A + A + I + I + T + T
B. A + A + A + I + T + T
C. A + I + I + I + T + T

Table 2 presents a DCP mezocycle made up of six microcycles structured according to sample A. This cycle cycle is designed for a runner aiming for a 3:45.0 1500.

Table 2

	Accumulation	Intensification	Transformation
Monday	CR_2 12km. 10 x 100m strides	CR_1 12km. 10 x 100 strides	CR_1 10 km.
Tuesday	Ext. int. 20 x 400m V=75s R=90s.	Int int. 10 x 400 V=60s R=3-4 min.	Race 1000m
Wednesday	CR_2 12 km.	CR_1 12 km.	CR_1 10 km.
Thursday	Ext. int. 20 x 400m V=75s R=90s	Tempo 4 x 600m V=1, 25 R=8 min.	Race 3000m
Friday	CR_1 15 km.	CR_1 12 km.	CR_1 10 km.
Saturday	Ext. int. 16 x 400m V=72s	Int int 10 x 400 V=60s R=3-4 min. R=3-4 min.	Race 800m
Sunday	Rest	Rest	Rest

CR_1 = continuous run at an easy pace HR = 140
CR_2 = continuous run at a moderate pace HR = 160
CR_3 = continuous run at a fast pace HR = 170-180

Ext. int. = Extensive intervals   V = speed of run
Int int. = Intensive intervals   R = rest periods

Each phase lasts for two weeks. All races in the transformation phase should occur at 90-95% maximum effort. The major competition should be scheduled three days after the last 800m control race.

Table 3

Day	Accumulation	Intensification	Transformation
Mon	L_2	L_2	L_2
Tues	L_3	L_2	L_1
Wed	L_2	L_3	L_2
Thurs	L_3	L_3	L_1
Fri	L_2	L_2	L_2
Sat	L_3	L_2	L_1
Sun	L_0	L_0	L_0

L stands for the training load and has three different values from low (L_1), through medium (L_2), to high (L_3). The DCP mesocycle should have the following order of training loads.

To ease planning and calculating the training load in the microcycles, use Table 4.

Table 4

Possibilities	Volume	Intensity	Training Load	Description
I	V_3 V_2 V_3	I_3 I_3 I_2	3	high training load
II	V_2 V_3 V_1	I_2 I_1 I_2	2	medium training load
III	V_1 V_1 V_2	I_1 I_1 I_1	1	low training load

Since the training load is the product of volume and intensity, this scheme helps to classify the load as high, medium and low. Research has shown that the proper proportions of volume and intensity in the DCP cycle are the key to reaching form at the desired time.

Table 5 shows four variations of volume distribution in a monthly mezocycle. The volume has been expressed in percent of total mileage.

Table 6 presents the intensity and volume in six consecutive microcycles of a DCP mezocycle.

Table 5

Variations	Consecutive Microcycles				Volume %
	1	2	3	4	
I	35	28	22	15	100
II	28	35	22	15	100
III	28	22	35	15	100
IV	35	15	28	22	100

The main goal of the DCP cycle is to direct the supercompensation phase of the athlete's body for the time of the major competition. The coach must remember that this physiological phenomenon will occur only if the balance between stimulus and rest is planned properly.

Proper rest periods between training sessions have to be maintained. The problem becomes even more complicated when two or three sessions take place daily.

Table 7

Levels of Volume and Intensity (1-3)	Rest Interval in Hours
V_1-V_2	4 hours
V_2-I_2	6 hours
V_3-I_1	8 hours
V_3-I_2	10 hours
V_3-I_3	12 hours

Table 7 presents the minimum values of rest for sessions of different volume and intensity.

Shorter rest periods will cause accumulation of stress and result in overtraining. It is advised that the number of consecutive days in which the training load is high (3 points) does not exceed six. For advanced runners 8-12 hours of rest should be taken between practice sessions and one day a week should be free of training.

Special attention should be given to biological renewal of the athlete's body. Physical and chemical therapy, diet, and psychological comfort greatly speed up the recuperation process.

Table 6: Six-week DCP mesocycle

Consecutive microcycles	I	II	III	IV	V	VI
Intensity expressed in % of race speed	80-90	90-95	75-100	105-110	110-115	100-105
Volume expressed in % of total mileage for the 6 weeks	3-12	80-20	20-40	40-20	22-8	8-2

To sum up the new concepts of training load distribution, we will present a few samples from top East German programs. The ability to prepare peak form at the desired time lies mainly in the proper distribution of volume and intensity in the macro, mezo and microcycles.

Graphs 2a and 2b compare two training cycles. In 2a too much intensity without adequate rest caused the form to decline after 10 days of training. The cycle had to be altered because of overtraining. Easy continuous runs had to be introduced for two weeks.

Graphs 2b and 2c present a properly planned mezocycle in which high intensity days were interspersed by days of medium or high volume training. The athlete's form developed properly.

Graphs 3 a-b-c show sample microcycles for a woman middle distance runner. The samples are from the 6th, 33rd and 35th microcycle of the annual plan. The training load (L_1, L_2, L_3) and character of training (general, specific) are included. 3b presents a cycle from the general preparation period, while 3b and 3c are the intensification and transformation phases of the DCP mezocycle. The runner set a personal record in the 800 with a 1:58.2 clocking.

The ideas presented give us a new look at the theory of training here, yet they do not solve all the problems. There are a few very successful schools of running in the world and each has a different approach, which means we are still far from optimal training procedures. This may irritate the scientists and coaches, yet to the fans and athletes it means world records will keep falling and faster times will keep coming in the future.

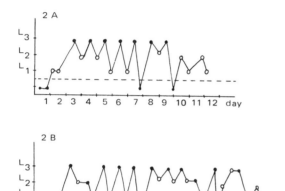

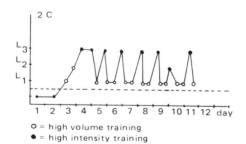

O = high volume training
● = high intensity training

GRAPHS 2a-b-c

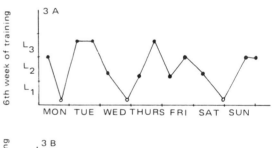

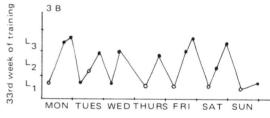

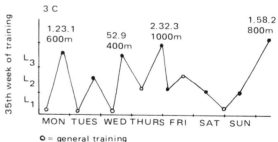

O = general training
● = special training

GRAPHS 3a-b-c

VARIATIONS IN MIDDLE DISTANCE RUNNING TRAINING

by Ray Lapinski, Australia

The author discusses various middle distance running methods and presents his views on a complex approach to training in situations where strict periodization is impractical.

When first developing a training program, I was heavily influenced by the work of Arthur Lydiard of New Zealand and Percy Cerutty of Australia. Both of these world famous coaches believe very strongly in yearly training cycles, or what is commonly known as periodization. Lydiard divided his year into a six-month marathon phase, a two-month hill phase, a two-month track phase, and a one-month racing phase. His intense psychological and physical training consisted of six months of conditioning and distance running, three months of race practice and three months of competition.

Having coached and studied various training methods in Australia, I realized that the Australians approach their five-month long cross country season as a strict preparation for the outdoor track season. Indoor track is nonexistent. The British and most other European nations have the same philosophy. In fact, the British AAA Cross Country Championships usually fall in late February, just two to three weeks before the World Cross Country Championships. They then begin what Lydiard would call the track phase. This would lead into the racing phase or season, which in Europe doesn't begin until late June and ends in early September.

In direct contrast, the Americans place almost equal emphasis on all three seasons. Consider the plight of the collegiate distance runner—NCAA Cross Country Championships in early November, TAC Cross Country Championships in late November, TAC Indoor Championships in late February, NCAA Indoor in March, NCAA outdoor in May, TAC outdoor in June and then, if he's good enough, there are the major international meets in August and early September. These athletes are either forced to peak three or four times a year, if concentrating on all three, or they are trying to hold a peak for perhaps a 14- to 16-week period, if the main emphasis is on outdoor track.

However, Costill (1979) states, ". . . the runner can repeat the quality of performance several times over a 3- to 4-week period." He further adds, ". . . tapering for peak performance may only prove useful once in a competitive season . . . and can only be revived again after a period of basic noncompetitive training and release from the psychological stress of competition." It's no wonder the Americans have performed so poorly in the distance events during major international meets.

THE COMPLEX METHOD

The Australian system has evolved because many of the Oceanic athletes are forced to compete out of season. This system allows them to remain at a reasonable competitive fitness level all year round. It must be emphasized that a strong aerobic background is required before undertaking this method of training. The only variation that occurs during the year would be a decrease in distance and intensity prior to major competitions.

The Australian or complex method, in direct contrast to Lydiard's or Cerutty's systems of periodization, is based on many types of training performed throughout a weekly or bi-weekly cycle. The two-week cycle, for example, would consist of two long aerobic runs, three or four interval sessions, two steady-state runs, a hill session and an easy recovery run.

The two-week cycle also incorporates Bill Bowerman's hard-easy concept. As Richard Amery (1974) stated, "It has been recognized by most discerning coaches and athletes in recent years that a judicious use of light training will bring more rapid results than continual hard work." Dr. James Counsilman of the University of Indiana and Australian Olympic swimming coach, Forbes Carlisle, have done a great deal of research in the area of recovery periods. A good part of their work has been applied effectively to running. Carlisle (1973) has stated that "the training load must be severe and must be applied frequently enough and with sufficient intensity to cause the body to adapt maximally to a particular activity." Carlisle further maintains that "recuperation periods are essential . . . a rhythmical cycle of exercise and recuperation should be established." Tschiene (1978) and Fowler (1983) have used the diagram below to illustrate the format of load, recovery and progression.

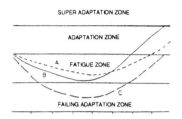

Figure 1: Super Adaptation (Counsilman, 1974)

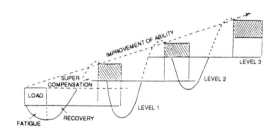

Figure 2: Load, Recovery and Progression Format (Tschiene, 1978)

Costill (1979) feels that overtraining and chronic fatigue can be directly related to muscle glycogen depletion. Dare (1979) states that "time is the essential factor in determining the degree of recovery and allowing for the proper adaptation to stress." He cites the work of Costill in saying that, after a day of a hard double workout , glycogen supplies may not be replenished for up to 48 hours. Dare maintains that a single hard anaerobic session can elevate blood lactate and deplete necessary enzymes for as long as 24 hours.

In developing my training program, I try to work on a hard-easy basis with some attention given to heart rate. The program includes the use of long aerobic runs, or what has commonly been called LSD (Long Slow Distance). These runs are done to attain fine muscular endurance. Lydiard (1983) quotes studies done at Cologne University in West Germany which show that these long runs expand neglected capillary beds and form new ones which serve to improve oxygen transport and use.

The bottom line in long runs is an increase in VO_2 max. However, as Dare (1979) states, "though the VO_2 max is a good indicator of aerobic ability, there are many individual differences that separate one runner from another. . ." He goes on to point out that the key seems to be that VO_2 max is important, but the ability to operate at a high percentage of VO_2 max is even more important.

ENERGY SYSTEMS

The point here is to develop our ability to operate at a much higher percentage. Bueno (1982) maintains, ". . . the ability to perform close to VO_2 max can be improved with training as much as 45% and some runners have shown the ability to reach 80 to 90% of their maximum. This ability to reach higher percentages can be achieved through more intense training procedures. Here it is necessary to have a thorough knowledge of the energy systems of the body and the athlete should be trained by tasks specific to the energy demands of the event.

In general, this means spending more time on the predominant energy systems. Bob Murray (1977), for example, suggests that the systems respond best in the following manner:

I. **The ATP-CP System**—repeats of maximum intensity and short duration with complete, passive rest and intervals of 120 seconds or more.
II. **The Lactic Acid (LA) System**—repeats of medium to hard intensity lasting one to four minutes, with an active rest to keep the burden on the LA system.
III. **The O_2 System**—repeats at 80% effort lasting over four minutes in duration with complete rest so as to keep LA levels at a minimum.

Canadian coach Brent McFarlane (1983) cites a lack of "universal and accurate terminology" in reference to energy systems and has attempted to simplify them by dividing them into the anaerobic lactate energy system, the aerobic energy system and the anaerobic alactic energy system. Here the anaerobic lactate system or glycolysis, has the accumulation of H + ions as the limiting factor. Intervals of 60 to 500m are used to shock the body and central nervous system with the accumulation of lactate terminating this system after 40 to 50 seconds. McFarlane suggests three types of training to properly educate this system. He calls these:

Special Endurance I—Repetitions at 90-100% for 20 to 40 seconds (150 to 300m). The workout should consist of 1 set of 1 to 5 reps, totaling 300 to 1200m, with complete recovery between reps (10 to 20 minutes). This training is race or competition specific.

Special Endurance II—Repetitions at 90 to 100% for 40 seconds to 2 minutes (300 to 600m). 1 to 3 reps, with complete recovery is indicated here. The recovery should be with easy jogging, or in a legs-up position to facilitate lactate removal.

Speed Endurance—Repetitions at 90 to 100% effort for 7 to 20 seconds (60 to 150m). The workout should consist of 2 to 3 sets of 2 to 5 reps, totaling 300 to 1200m with 2 to 5 minute recovery and 8 to 10 minutes between sets. Motor unit educability seems to be the primary purpose here.

These types of training are also suggested by McFarlane for the development of the aerobic energy system. These include:

Australian's middle distance star Simon Doyle

I. **Continuous Tempo**—long runs at 40 to 80% intensity.
II. **Extensive Tempo**—relaxed, smooth running at 60 to 80% with active recoveries.
III. **Intensive Tempo**—running at 80-90% with a relaxed, smooth and controlled tempo. At this level 6 to 12 reps are done with an active rest. This type of training is very close to speed endurance and special endurance training.

Research shows us that specific training of the predominant energy systems will increase the efficiency and endurance of each system, thus enabling the athlete to perform at a higher rate over a longer period of time. Henson (1981) points out that the body, training at maximum output, will show an increase in lactate production because the body is "better able to tolerate and continue running with high levels of lactic acid in the system."

Clohessy and Telford (1984) advocate the use of relaxed speed training. "It makes more sense to supplement your long, steady runs with 400's around the threshold level so that the set can be performed with quite brief recovery periods." This point is brought out by examining the energy requirements of the individual distance events and in the work of Henson (1981), who points out that the "greatest heart efficiency is at about 150 beats per minute; increases beyond this rate actually result in a decreased stroke volume due to the lack of filling time. . ."

TRACK WORKOUTS

Keeping in mind the above-mentioned principles of training, this author established a program of three track workouts that are utilized in each session all year round.

1. *Repetition 400m.* 10 to 20 reps, depending on the fitness level and the system to be stressed. For example, 20 x 400m in 80 seconds with quick 100m jog recoveries is strictly an O_2 workout. On the other hand, 3 sets of 4 reps, in which cut-downs (78,76,74,72 seconds) take place with quick 200m recoveries and the last four are performed considerably faster, represents combination energy systems training.

2. *Repetition miles.* 1 to 5 reps of one mile covered progressively faster. For example, 5:30 to 5:40—5:25 to 5:35—5:20 to 5:30—5:10 to 5:20—4:55 to 5:15, with slow 400m jog recoveries. The pace depends on the time of the year and the level of fitness. This workout serves

to train the aerobic system (intensive tempo).

3. *Three-kilometer workout.* Because of its nature, this is possibly the best workout. It is an excellent fitness indicator, as well as event specific, utilizing a fast start, surging and a hard finish. A number of energy systems are combined in covering 600m hard (1:40 to 1:55)—400m (88 to 90 seconds)—600m hard—800m (2:55 to 3:00)—600m hard.

We are looking for good hard, but relaxed 600's, as well as the total 3000m time being run at prerecorded pace. At the start of the year the total time may be around 10:25, in the middle of the year 10:00, before moving to a double 3km (1600m recovery) and getting to the point where both are in the 10:00-10:15 range. As we get closer to our peak racing period the workout is moved back to a single 3km, hitting this in the 9:30 to 9:40 range.

On occasion, just prior to the shorter, more important races, the 400m workouts incorporate 200's. This is done by doing eight reps of in and out 200's, followed by an active recovery of 800m. We then cut down to 8 x 200m with easy recoveries of slow 200m. Finally, we do 2-4 x 200m with complete recoveries.

One hill workout per cycle is also included in the program. For most of the year this workout would entail a hard run up a hill of 100 to 150m in length (medium grade), with a flat 50 to 75m hard effort at the top. Ideally we should be able to come down at a slight enough angle so as to reduce the stress on the knees. Anywhere from 8-20 reps are performed, depending on the grade of the hill and fitness level.

As we near the peaking period, the hill workout is shortened to 40-50m and performed with exaggerated bounding, rather than strict running. For the middle distance runners this peaking period will incorporate ATP-CP workouts in place of the hill workouts. A sample of this type of workout would include 2 to 3 sets of 5 reps of "finishes" that involve a gradual acceleration off the curve, so as to be at all out for approximately 60m of the straight. There is a full recovery between reps (slow walk back to start), and 8 to 10 minutes between sets. This workout actually places emphasis mostly on the anaerobic alactic energy system, with benefits accruing to the education of the motor units.

TRAINING METHODS IN THE 800 METERS

by Olav Karikosk, Estonia

The author discusses the distribution of aerobic, aerobic-anaerobic and anaerobic training methods employed by 800m world record holders and Olympic champions, divided into three categories according to the performance in their secondary events.

Performances in middle and long distance running have improved considerably during the last decades. There are many reasons for the improvement, most of them to be found in the changes of training methods. However, even the existing knowledge and experience has not been able to solve all training problems. Among these problems is the choice of inter-related training methods for a particular distance.

Many years ago well-known German authority, Toni Nett, divided middle and long distance training methods into five categories: 1) endurance runs, 2) extensive interval runs, 3) repetition runs, 4) sprinting, 5) strength training. This division has lately been changed to a classification based on energy production processes and divided into aerobic, aerobic-anaerobic and anaerobic methods.

Aerobic endurance development methods include continuous running, mostly in a steady-state situation where the oxygen intake and consumption are balanced. According to Pisuke and Nurmekivi, the blood lactate in the steady-state runs is around 27 to 36 mg%, the oxygen consumption about 50 to 70% from the maximum and the pulse rate 130 to 160 a minute. The aim is to improve the economy of the cardiovascular system and metabolism in order to lift the steady-state runnning pace.

The running pace is considerably faster in the

TABLE 1: Performances of the athletes under observation.

Rudolf Harbig (Germany)	Set a world record (1:46.6) that lasted 16 years in 1939.	100m—10.6; 400m—46.0 (world record), 1000m 2:21.5 (world record)
Mal Whitfield (USA)	Olympic champion 1948 and 1952.	800m—1:47.9; 100m—10.6; 400m—45.9.
Roger Moens (Belgium)	World record 1:45.7 in 1955. Olympic silver in 1960.	100m—11.3; 400m—47.3; mile—3:58.9.
Tom Courtney (USA)	Olympic champion 1956.	800m—1:45.8; 100m—10.6; 400m—45.8.
Peter Snell (New Zealand)	Olympic champion 1960 and 1964.	800m—1:44.3 (world record); 100m—11.3; 400m—47.7; mile—3:54.1 (world record).
Ralph Doubell (Australia)	Olympic champion 1968.	800m—1:44.3 (eq. world record); 400m—46.4; mile—4:00.6.
David Wottle (USA)	Olympic champion 1972.	800m—1:44.4 (eq. world record); 100m—11.7; 1500m—3:36.2; mile—3:53.3.
Marcello Fiasconaro (Italy)	World record 1:43.7 in 1973.	100m—10.5; 4300m—45.5.
Alberto Juantorena (Cuba)	Olympic champion 1976.	800m—1:43.44 (world record); 400m—44.26; 100m—10.4; 200m—20.8.
Steve Ovett (Britain)	Olympic champion 1980.	800m—1:44.10; 200m—21.7; 400m—47.5; 1500m—3:30.77 (world record).
Sebastian Coe (Britain)	World record 1:41.74 in 1980.	400m—46.87; 1000m—2:12.18 (world record); 1500m—3:31.95 (world record): mile—3:347.33 (world record).
Joaquim Cruz (Brazil)	Olympic champion 1984.	800m—1:41.77, 400m—47.27; 1500m—3:36.48.
Willi Wulbeck (Germany)	World champion 1983.	800m—1:43.65; 400m—47.27: 1500m—3:33.74.

use of *aerobic-anaerobic* training methods, involving anaerobic energy production processes. The blood lactate concentration reaches 37 to 80 mg%, the oxygen consumption is 70 to 100% from the maximum and the pulse rate 160 to 190 a minute. The aim is to develop maximum aerobic power and the methods employed include fast endurance runs, fartlek and extensive interval runs close to racing speed.

Anaerobic training methods consist of fast runs involving a large oxygen debt. The lactate concentration exceeds 80 mg% and the pulse rate is over 190 a minute. The methods employed include intensive interval runs at the racing speed or faster, repetition runs and sprints. Strength training, jumping exercises, bounding, etc. are also classified as anaerobic methods.

PERFORMANCES

Let's now look at the training methods used by 800m world record holders and Olympic champions beginning with Rudolf Harbig and including 1983 world champion Willi Wulbeck. The performances of these athletes are presented in Table 1, the distribution of their training methods in Table 2.

METHODS

The 800m Olympic champions and world record holders can be divided into three groups. The first includes athletes whose second event is the 400m and who have also achieved good performances (10.4 to 10.6) in the 100m (Harbig, Whitfield, Courtney, Fiasconaro, Juantorena). The second group includes athletes with a more or less equal 400 and 1500m performances (Moens, Doubell). The third group is made up from runners who have the 1500m for their other basic event but are relatively poor over 400m (Snell, Wottle, Ovett, Cruz, Wulbeck, Coe).

As can be seen in Table 2, the first group has the lowest aerobic training volume. Surprising is that Harbig, who trained only 3 or 4 times a week, had his largest volume in this group. The lowest aerobic volumes belong to Courtney and Juantorena. Juantorena, who trained 6 times a week, obviously wasn't interested in a large running volume.

The largest mixed aerobic-anaerobic training volume belongs to Juantorena and Fiasconaro. Harbig began anaerobic work only in April, while all other athletes in the first group included anaerobic training in their programs during the preparation

TABLE 2: The distribution of training methods of the world record holders and Olympic champions.

Athlete		Average Weekly Training Volumes (km)		
		Aerobic	Aerobic-Anaerobic	Anaerobic
Harbig	P.	30	11.5	---
	C.	25	2.1	2.3
Whitfield	P.	27	11.0	2.6
	C.	22	2.8	4.2
Moens	P.	65	5.8	2.8
	C.	31	3.4	5.6
Courtney	P.	21	13.2	1.8
	C.	15	1.2	4.5
Snell	P.	126	32.0	---
	C.	36	18.0	5.8
Danbell	C.	45	16.0	3.4
Wottle	P.	84	53.0	0.8
	C.	59	10.4	5.3
Fiasconaro	P.	29	18.8	3.7
	C.	20	8.4	5.2
Juantorena	P.	21	20.4	3.5
	C.	19	7.0	6.5
Ovett	P.	99	47.0	2.9
	C.	28	23.0	4.6
Cruz	P.	56	44.0	0.8
	C.	40	1.2	7.2
Wulbeck	P.	66	66.0	1.0
	C.	32	21.0	5.7
Coe	P.	72	24.0	2.4
	C.	32	33.0	6.4

P = Preparation period   C = Competition period

period.

Juantorena and Fiasconaro trained with their largest volume and highest intensity in winter. Fiasconaro did 300m repetitions in 37 seconds with walk recoveries, Juantorena twice a week 200m repetitions in the 23.6 to 23.8 seconds range. Both exceeded the previous world record holders in their volume and intensity of aerobic-anaerobic, as well as anaerobic work.

Moens in the second group was the first to better Harbig's legendary world mark thanks mainly to his endurance training. He experimented several years with different methods and finally reached the conclusion that an emphasis on endurance development suited him best. His aerobic work volume reached up to 80km a week. Snell, who eliminated Moens from the world record list, doubled Moen's training volume, while Doubell apparently had the highest intensity in this group.

Athletics in the third group are identified by their large aerobic training volume. The largest aerobic volume was employed by Snell and Ovett, the largest aerobic-anaerobic volume by Wottle, Ovett and Cruz. Snell didn't use anaerobic training during the first 10 weeks in the preparation period, while Cruz ran in winter 10 x 400m in 61 to 62 seconds with 60 to 90 second recoveries. The last can be regarded as aerobic-anaerobic, as it was well below racing pace. Ovett and Coe employed also in winter a limited volume of sprinting over 60 to 200m distances.

The most intensive training during the competition period was used by Cruz, Ovett and Coe. Cruz, for example, performed 22 to 23 second 200m repetitions and 50 to 51 second 400m repetitions with 200m jog recoveries. Ovett covered 12 to 200m in 26 seconds with 15 second recoveries; Coe performed 4 to 5 repetitions of 800m below 1.50 minutes, etc.

The athletes in the third group didn't follow in Snell's footsteps. The total training volume dropped to 60km a week for Coe, while Cruz's and Wulbeck's volumes were around 100km. However, their volumes and intensities in aerobic-anaerobic and anaerobic work have increased considerably. The main training methods employed in the aerobic-anaerobic combination include, besides fartlek and fast cross-cointry runs, extensive interval training, using 600m, 400, 300 and 1000m during the preparation period and 600, 400, 800 and 300m distances during the competition period.

The pace in interval training is generally increased from month to month until it reaches racing speed prior to the competition period and turns into anaerobic work. The most common anaerobic training methods during the preparation period include 200, 100 and 300m repetitions, during the competition period 200, 400 and 600m distances. Dominating is the 200m distance.

VARIATIONS

Harbig, Whitfield, Courtney, Doubell, Fiasconaro, Juantorena, Cruz and Coe placed considerable emphasis on strength development. They used, besides uphill runs and bounding, also barbell exercises. Moens, Snell, Ovett and Wulbeck restricted themselves only to uphill running.

The first group found it most suitable to run in training relatively fast with long recoveries and a limited number of repetitions. The nervous and muscular structures of the athletes in this group appear to tolerate fast work better in the anaerobic zone because their muscular metabolism is not sufficiently economical to delay fatigue. Consequently an increased training volume will have a negative influence on their performances.

Athletes in the second group train with similar or slightly reduced intensity but employ shorter recoveries and a larger number of repetitions. Their metabolism, in comparison to the first group, is more economical and helps to delay the onset of fatigue.

The third group employs the largest volume of aerobic, as well as aerobic-anaerobic, training methods. Their anaerobic training intensity is close to that of the other two groups. Athletes in the third group appear to have the most economical metabolism. Consequently they train much slower and employ shorter recoveries between repetitions.

SUMMARY

1. Emphasis in 800m training should be placed on the development of the dominating performance capacities of an athlete. It appears that a more intensive but smaller training volume is suitable for faster middle distance runners, a larger volume for endurance-type athletes.

2. The development of the weaker performance capacities should not be completely overlooked. Fast middle distance runners need to pay attention, besides specific endurance, also to the development of general endurance. Endurance-type 800m runners, on the other hand, should not overlook the development of speed and specific endurance.

3. The training intensity has increased in all three groups but the total volume in aerobic training has been somewhat reduced.

MONITORING CLUB LEVEL MIDDLE DISTANCE RUNNERS FOR OVERTRAINING

by Peter Good, Australia

Monitoring is an important aspect in the evaluation of tolerance and recovery in middle distance running training. In the following text Peter Good presents some observations on how simple monitoring methods can help to prevent overtraining under overloading training procedures.

Training is only beneficial when it forces the body to adapt to the stress of the given load. If the stress is not sufficient to overload the body, then no adaptation will take place. The "principle of overload" states that habitually overloading a system will cause it to respond and adapt, thus producing an increased performance. If athletes were to undergo the same training load and intensity each year then performances would stagnate.

There is one exception to this rule and that is of the junior athlete. Improvements in performance will be forthcoming in these formative years without training increases due to growth and adaptation of the developing organism. Overload should not be a feature of the junior athlete's program.

ADAPTATION

Thus, the application of stress is fundamental to improve performance. It must be specific to the event and to the individual athlete. The "General Adaptation Syndrome" by Dr. Hans Seyle explains the physiological response and adaptation to stress in three stages:

1. Alarm reaction—the initial response to the stressor. This activates the sympathetic nervous system which in essence brings tremendous amounts of glucose and oxygen to the organs to combat the stress. It is the "fight or flight" reflex that involves the mobilization of systems and processes through various hormones.

2. Resistance development—in this stage the body is primed and fueled to resist stress. Improvements in capacity are now achieved due to the adaptive response of the organism, provided the stress is tolerable.

3. Exhaustion—when the stress becomes intolerable the organism becomes distressed and breaks down through failure to adapt.

It is important to note here that the general adaptation syndrome is the reaction of the organism in defense to any stressor. Stressors occur throughout our lifetime in many different ways, i.e., emotional, medical, physical and so on. The general adaptation syndrome does not recognize a difference between any of these stresses.

OVERLOAD

Overload can be administered by increasing the training volume or the training intensity. Both are integral components of the preparation phase (volume) and the pre-competition phase (intensity) respectively.

Training volume consists of training frequency and duration. The training volume can be increased by implementing extra sessions, or sessions can be extended to cover extra distance. In both instances an increase in *quantity* is the method of overload. Training intensity is the level of effort required for the work load. This can be increased by reducing recovery periods or increasing speed. In this instance an increase in *quality* is the method of overload. As mentioned earlier, stress can manifest itself in many forms other than physical (through training), and therefore this must be taken into consideration as an extra overload affecting the organism. Psychologists label this life stress and the stressors are caused through everyday circumstances, i.e., work and family environments, weather, moods, etc. These can markedly affect the intra-relationship of training sessions without being evident at the time.

An example of this is when an athlete arrives at training having already been subjected to work stress. Energy levels are then reduced and therefore effort levels will be higher to perform the training session. It is possible that this stress can manifest itself by a poor training performance. Usually, however, due to the enhanced physical condition of the athlete, it would take a major stress to affect one training session. The more inherent problem is when this situation goes undetected for some time and has a cumulating effect of fatigue.

OVERTRAINING

Overtraining is the end product of the overload in a training program due to failed adaptation, the third stage of the general adaptation syndrome—exhaustion. It is basically caused through an imbalance between the overload and the recovery components in the program. Exhaustion can manifest itself in two forms, of which the acute and chronic form (overuse) include stress fractures, emotional problems, illness and numerous soft tissue injuries.

Sport medicine has a large number of procedures for the diagnosis of fatigue and overtraining. However, these are costly, need special equipment and the services of a qualified sport physiologist. It is therefore imperative that the coach is capable of making symptomatic evaluations.

There are well documented signs, subjective and objective, to indicate the possibility of overtraining:

Subjective

- Loss of appetite
- General feeling of lethargy, loss of enthusiasm for training (weak motivation)
- Mood changes, increased irritation
- Insomnia
- Disordered bowel habits
- Increased susceptibility to illness and injury
- Generalized muscle and joint pain
- Injury.

Objective

- Decreased performance
- Weight loss (reduced body fat)
- Increased resting and recovery heart rates
- Decreased blood pressure

- Blood hematology imbalances (i.e., low ferritin, cpk, hematrocrit).

MONITORING

The majority of these symptoms, with the exception of decreased performance, may not stand out at supervised training sessions. The athletes may be able to raise themselves for the training session, but throughout the rest of the day it may be a different story. For this reason the author decided to compile an athlete monitor assessment sheet to be filled out weekly (Table 1).

Table 1: Monitoring Assessment Sheet

The items listed on the sheet are simple to carry out, do not need expensive equipment, give immediate feedback which should be acted upon by either the coach or the athlete, and are objective when evaluated in conjunction with the training program.

The first three items are the athletes' subjective evaluations of:

Control—did the athlete feel in control of the training sessions, i.e., was the effort level paced

91

throughout the session in accordance with the set work or did the session control him?

Mental Application—were concentration and motivation optimum, were they able to mentally, as well as physically apply themselves to the set tasks?

Recovery—did they feel recovery was adequate between sessions? Obviously in overload periods this item becomes important, as full recovery does not happen until recovery weeks are programmed.

The next two items, nutrition and sleep, evaluate whether food and rest requirements were adequate for the training load. These are key factors that become increasingly important during the overload. Without adequate food for fuel, and sleep for recovery, the athletes will exhaust their reserves.

Heart Rate—the resting pulse has been well documented as an indicator of physical abnormalities. This is normally taken first thing in the morning and is called the basal rate. Rises of five beats per minute are said to indicate increased susceptibility to overtraining or illness.

OBSERVATIONS

Heart Rate

A point of great consideration when evaluating daily heart rate is that at rest and during low-intensity submaximal work the rate can be influenced by numerous factors, such as anxiety, dehydration, temperature, altitude, alcohol, etc. For this reason an am/pm (first thing in the morning and last at night) heart rate monitoring can be recommended. This, the author feels, would give a thorough evaluation of the recovery process from training and also might help to appraise external influences.

All the athletes monitored in this way by the author became aware of their responses to work and recovery. The golden standard of the morning heart rate increases of more than five beats a minute did not appear to be an accurate predictor of impending problems, as daily fluctuations well in excess occur without affecting performance or being indicative of problems.

Heart rate monitoring incorporated during training sessions appears to be a more accurate daily indicator than the basal rate. They are recorded at set increments during the recovery periods. With overstress the maximal heart rate is achieved earlier and the recovery will not be as fast.

Weight

Weight drops, specifically post-workouts, are associated with an increased risk of injury or illness. Weight reduction will be encountered when extra training is involved and should not be confused with overtraining. This condition should be evaluated with other symptoms.

Iron Deficiency

A cause for concern, particularly in endurance events, is iron deficiency and anemia. The term "sport anemia" has been defined as "a hemoglobin level below normal, associated with low iron stores in the absence of recognized disease process."

For monitoring purposes the hemoglobin content alone would not be sufficient or safe. A blood iron study test recording serum ferritin, iron store, TIBC, percent saturation and hemoglobin would be more useful.

Because the recorded measurements are related to a normal range, it does not necessarily mean an athlete in the lower end of this range is at risk. It seems to be more objective to establish base levels and then monitor for decreases than it is to just be concerned with the normal range. However, those in the lower end should be singled out and extra consideration given with regard to the observation of recovery and effort levels.

To effectively combat this problem I would suggest that a blood iron test be performed before major overload periods. Any athlete recording low on normal range should then supplement accordingly. A second test is taken at the completion of the overload cycle to indicate exactly what effect, if any, it had on the iron status. As the latent stage appears to be the stage that affects performance, the identification of athletes in the pre-latent stage would facilitate early supplementation to avoid the ensuing problems.

SUMMARY

The art of coaching is to provide the optimal amounts of intensity and quantity without exceeding the tolerance and recovery capacity of the athlete. Monitoring is very important in evaluating tolerance and recovery limits. It gives greater control through increased awareness to symptoms and abnormalities. There must be a multi-faceted approach in this area as shown in Figure 1. As can be seen, if the coach is able to recognize the early symptoms, the athlete can be sent directly to the appropriate specialist. This eliminates wasted time by referrals.

When overtraining problems become evident,

immediate action should be taken. This does not mean an abrupt end to training. When an athlete has been subjecting his body to a given daily stress, it can be assumed that he is continually in the resistance stage of the general adaptation syndrome. If training is suspended then it is possible that it could force the organism into the alarm reaction. "Sudden rest is as large a stress in a negative direction as is the overload" (Dr. L. Kipke 1985). This syndrome is not widely understood at present but can be observed during recovery weeks when the load has been too light and athletes complain of feeling subjectively tired and lethargic.

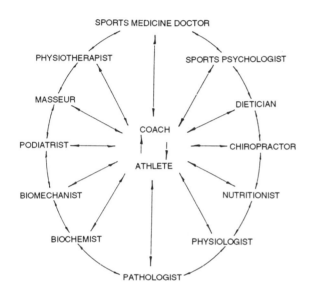

Figure 1: Multi-Faceted Approach To Coaching Appropriate Specialists Eliminate Errors

While athletes are keen to physically train and follow training programs they can be dispassionate when filling in assessment sheets. It is a difficult problem to solve with a 100% success rate without bringing in Draconian measures. However, by taking the initial steps of educating the athletes to the evaluation of overtraining signs, they are at least aware of the problems.

The important aspect of monitoring is that it identifies the individual athlete's "normal" physiological characteristics. Deviations from these are recognized as warning signals of likely problems. If this area is not addressed properly, then with overtraining it becomes a case of shutting the gate after the horse has bolted.

The coach's role is fundamental in monitoring the athlete. It is not just a question of training that produces the physical performance. If success is to be achieved, a holistic approach to athlete care must be implemented, which would then enable both the athlete and the coach to achieve personal fulfillment.

REFERENCES

1. Brooks, G.A. and Fahey, T.D. (1984). *Exercise Physiology*.
2. Clement, D.B. and Asmundson, R.C. (1982). "Nutritional Intake and Hematological Parameters in Endurance Runners." *Physician and Sports Medicine*, 10(3).
3. Clement, D.B. and Sawchuk, L.L. (1984). "Iron Status and Sports Performance." *Sports Medicine*, 1(1).
4. Fricker, P., Clarke, F., Telford, R., Kupkee, W., Beasley, S. (1985). "Sports Anemia and the 'At Risk' Athlete." *Sports Science and Medicine Quarterly*, 1(3).
5. Javorek, I. (1987), "Methods to Enhance Recovery and Avoid Overtraining." *NSCA Journal*. 9(3).
6. Hughson, R. (1986). "Distance Athlete Monitoring." Canadian Track and Field Association Coaches Symposium.
7. Kipke, L. (1986). "The Importance of Recovery After Training and Competitive Efforts." *Track Technique #98*.
8. Kuipers, H. and Keizer, H.A. (1988). "Overtraining in Elite Athletes." *Sports Medicine*, 6(56).
9. McKenzie, D.C. and Newhouse, I. (1987). "Monitoring the Elite Athlete." The Oceania Track and Field Coaching Conference, Wellington, New Zealand.
10. Meitern, K. (1989). "Overtraining and The Role Of Pharmacology." *Modern Athlete and Coach*, 27(1).
11. Ryan, A.J., Brown, R.L., Burke, E.R., et. al. (1983). "Round Table: Overtraining In Athletics." *Physician and Sports Medicine*, 11(6).
12. Selye, H. (1976). *The Stress of Life*. McGraw-Hill.

CHAPTER IV

THE YOUNG MIDDLE DISTANCE RUNNER

SOME FACTORS INFLUENCING THE TRAINING OF YOUNG MIDDLE DISTANCE RUNNERS

by Alfred Pisuke and Ants Nurmekivi, Estonia

The authors look at the major aspects to be considered in the planning of training for young middle distance runners in the 10 to 18 years age range.

SPECIFIC FACTORS

Despite several basic similarities with the training of adults, there are a number of factors to be considered in the preparation of young distance runners. The most important of these specific factors are:

- Consideration of the specific age features
- Employing the principle of a proportional development of physical capacities
- The use of training means and methods that lead to the development of a foundation for future top performances
- The development of different physical capacities during the optimal development age
- Turning training into an emotional and interesting activity.

The age specific features from the viewpoint of endurance training include two most important indicators in the aerobic and anaerobic work capacities. Looking at oxygen consumption shows that differences between adult and young athletes exist only in their absolute values. There is no difference in the O_2 consumption for kilogram of body weight. Theoretically children have the same endurance capacity as adults, however, this is not exactly true in practice. The reason for this is first in the much higher maximal heart frequency of children. The high heart rate reduces the stroke volume and increases the recovery time after work.

Despite this, there is no indication today that the development of the functional capacities of children should be limited. There is danger only in overloading that can lead to disturbances in the nervous system. It is therefore most important during the growth period to take into consideration the need for more time to recover from training.

The anaerobic work capacity of young athletes, in comparison to their aerobic work capacity, is lower. It appears that this is partly influenced by hormonal factors. However, it should be stressed that training allows the significant improvement of the anaerobic work capacity, particularly in the 14 to 18 years age range (Kindermann). According to Travini, the most suitable age to begin with the development of general endurance is 9 to 10 years. The development of specific endurance for boys should start at the age of 14 to 15 years, for girls 13 to 14 years.

At the same time it is important that the development of all physical capacities must take place in proportion and distance runners are no exception. Besides the development of endurance, young distance runners must not forget the development of speed, strength, flexibility, mobility, coordination and so on. The development of general all-round physical capacities must also be in proportion to the improvement of specific capacities.

The correct planning of training from youth into adulthood should take a wave-like step-by-step increased workload that incorporates gradually the most efficient training means. The wavy pattern is organized to develop different physiological systems during their most suitable periods, reducing the load at the less effective ages.

Because middle and long distance running depends largely on the oxygen transport system, it is useful to incorporate in the training program, in addition to endurance runs, other activities of similar influence, such as skiing and swimming. This applies in particular to the first non-specific phase of training where a large number of different means are used to develop the aerobic work capacity.

TRAINING PHASES

The training of young distance runners is usually divided into three main development phases, known as the preliminary, first specialization and main specialization phases. According to Filini the three phases are based on the following developmental model:

PRELIMINARY PHASE (12 TO 14 YEARS)

Basic tasks: 1. All-round physical development. 2. Establishment of the basic techniques in running and other track and field events. 3. Development of general endurance. 4. Development of speed.

Basic training means: 1. Movement and sport games. 2. Different sporting activities that are related to endurance. 3. Steady-state endurance runs. 4. Sprinting.

Training load: General endurance development—30 to 40km a week, 120 to 140km a month, 900 to 1000km a year.

FIRST SPECIALIZATION PHASE (15 TO 16 YEARS)

Basic tasks: 1. All-round physical development. 2. Development of general endurance. 3. Improvement of running technique. 4. Development of speed. 5. Development of specific endurance. 6. Development of power.

Basic training means: 1. Steady-state endurance runs. 2. Running at alternating speeds. 3. Sprinting. 4. Different sporting activities that develop endurance.

Training load: General endurance development—50 to 60km a week, 2200km a year. Specific endurance development—220km a year.

MAIN SPECIALIZATION PHASE (17 TO 18 YEARS)

Basic Tasks: 1. Development of specific endurance. 2. Development of general endurance. 3. Development of speed.

Basic training means: 1. Steady-state endurance runs. 2. Running at alternating speeds. 3. Sprinting.

Training load: General endurance development—90 to 100km a week, 3500km a year. Specific endurance development—310km a year.

It should be noted that the pace of endurance runs in the preliminary training phase must be carefully chosen. It is recommended that the coach select the pace so that both halves of a reasonably long distance are covered at the same speed. Children in their first training year run 3km in about 20 minutes, in the second year 4km in 25 minutes and in the third year 5km in 27 minutes. Recoveries are checked by pulse rates, which should drop below 120 beats a minutes within five minutes after the run.

FACTORS FOR CONSIDERATION

A few sessions of repetition runs can be included in the training plan of this phase. Distances for the repetition runs are selected from short (80 to 100m), medium (150 to 300m) and long (600 to 1000m) runs, with walking recoveries that allow the pulse rate to drop below 120 before the next repetition is performed. The speed is increased when the young athlete is capable of running the last repetition faster than the previous repetitions. The total length of the repetitions should correspond with the length of the planned competition distance.

Specific training means are gradually introduced in the first specialization phase with the aim to develop, among other aspects, the capacity to maintain critical speed. Training continues to be many-sided without forgetting power development. There is a natural improvement of the anaerobic work capacity during this phase but care must be taken not to force it. Recoveries after anaerobic work must be adequate and this should be completely eliminated from the training program when the athlete is frequently involved in racing.

Specific training means are predominant in the main specialization phase when training includes all the methods used by adult athletes. More and more attention is given to anaerobic glycolitic training means but care is needed to ensure that the volume of these means does not exceed that of adult athletes. Care is also needed to secure an adequate recovery after this type of workout.

The planning of training is in general based on finding an optimal balance between aerobic, aerobic-anaerobic and anaerobic work. Most dangerous here can be excessive anaerobic-training, as well as over-forced volumes of aerobic running. Recoveries play an important part in the training. Medium loads that allow recovery by the next day are preferable. Two days, or even more, are needed for recovery after heavy work loads. Maxsimenko, for example, recommends the following planning of microcycles in the first specialization phase:

PREPARATION PERIOD

Monday	—	general endurance
Tuesday	—	speed and strength training
Wednesday	—	recovery
Thursday	—	general endurance
Friday	—	speed and specific endurance
Saturday	—	recovery
Sunday	—	recovery

COMPETITION PERIOD

Monday	—	specific endurance
Tuesday	—	speed and strength training
Wednesday	—	recovery
Thursday	—	speed and general endurance
Friday	—	specific endurance
Saturday	—	recovery
Sunday	—	recovery

How the various basic training means are distributed in a multi-year training plan of young middle and long distance runners is shown in Table 1. According to Travini the volume for girls is expected to be about 20% smaller on an average. The figures in Table 1 correspond closely with the recommendations of other authors, including Logvinov, who recommends that 75% of the total training volume should be devoted to running in the aerobic critical intensity zone, 20% in the aerobic-anaerobic zone and 5% in the above-critical aerobic zone. Logvinov claims that this approach is in the long-term more efficient than using 50% of the total volume for aerobic training, 30% for aerobic-anaerobic and 20% anaerobic running. The last appears to bring fast improvements in the 10 to 14 years age group but was later responsible for significantly poorer development.

As far as running speed is concerned in different types of training sessions, the speeds given by Finland's coach Seppanen for 1000m splits will provide some guidance in Table 2.

IN CONCLUSION

From the above-listed factors, scientific research and practical experience the recommended distance running training can be summed up in three major points, as follows:

1. Preparation in the early training phases can bring success without employing high intensity training means that can lead to performance stagnation later.
2. The use of many-sided general endurance and speed development in the first two training phases creates a foundation for specific training means in the following phases.
3. It is not recommended to begin specific training for top performance before the age of 18 years (girls a year or two earlier).

Table 1: The distribution of basic training means in a multi-year development program of young distance runners (Travini).

AGE (YEARS)	RUNNING SPEED AND VOLUME							
	AEROBIC		AEROBIC-ANAEROBIC		ANAEROBIC			TOTAL VOLUME (km)
	1	2	3	4	5	6	7	
10-11	288	180	60	36	24	6	6	600
11-12	378	310	87	65	35	15	10	900
13-14	432	514	142	79	56	24	18	1265
15-16	563	737	229	132	118	32	29	1860
17-18	929	1228	456	208	144	41	37	3043

1=low intensity; 2=moderate intensity; 3=tempo cross-country runs; 4=long aerobic-anaerobic runs; 5=racing speed; 6=faster then arcing speed; 7=close to maximal speed.

Table 2: Suggested running speeds in the training of young distance runners (boys).

AGE (YEARS)	DISTANCE (KM)	SLOW ENDURANCE RUN	MEDIUM ENDURANCE RUN	TEMPO CROSS-COUNTRY
15-16	3-5	4:35-5:00	4:15-4:30	3:55-4:00
	6-9	4:45-5:15	4:25-4:45	4:05-4:15
	10-15	4:55-5:30	4:35-5:00	4:15-4:30
	4-7	4:25-4:45	4:05-4:15	3:45-3:55
17-18	8-11	4:35-5:00	4:15-4:30	3:55-4:00
	12-18	4:45-5:15	4:25-4:45	4:05-4:15
	5-9	4:15-4:30	3:55-4:00	3:30-3:40

OPTIMIZATION OF THE TRAINING LOAD IN MIDDLE DISTANCE RUNNING

by Joachim Raczek, Poland

A rational distribution of training loads is particularly important in the long-term development of young athletes. The following text presents detailed models for an optimal load and intensity distribution of middle distance runners in the 13 to 19 years age range.

1. THE PROBLEM

Athletic training is a complex process for the development of the human organism's adaptation capacities by means of steadily increasing loads. The success of training is not only dependent on the volume of the loads, but also on their character, type and structure. For this reason the problem of a rational distribution of loads within long-term training processes becomes particularly important.

The model demands decisions here regarding the direction of the target parameters for the determination of the work in the single training phases. The analysis of high performance training and the construction of loads in each training phase rests not only on the determination and distribution of training loads. It is essential to take into consideration the principles of an optimal development of the organism. We are therefore not only dealing with the determination of the total workload for each training phase but considering the developmental peculiarities of young athletes, as well as the specific demands of a particular event. Only a model, based on established criteria and fixed norms for loading, allows the planning of rational training.

Solving these problems in practice is difficult and complex. The difficulties are mainly in the correct recognition of the volume and the structure of the loads and the establishment of an efficient system of these loads in the process of long-term training.

2. THE STUDY METHOD

The procedures presented in this text are base don long-term studies of the dynamics of metabolism, as well as an analysis of the training of young athletes over several years. The dynamics of metabolism included blood lactate values in different load formats, as the practical use of lactate diagnostics for an optimal guidance of training processes has been confirmed in numerous studies.

Several components that decide the lactate concentration were taken into consideration. These included the intensity of the load, threshold values and lactate curve profiles, as well as maximal values. The procedures allowed the establishment of a better insight into these correlations.

The results of the studies in the laboratory and under field conditions (during training and after races) allow the classification of training loads for young athletes (Table 1). This classification takes into consideration six intensity ranges within three energy zones—aerobic, mixed and anaerobic.

The first range covers mainly compensating loads and loads used for the maintenance of the achieved training stage. The second range includes developmental loads that do not exceed the 4 mmol/l anaerobic threshold value. The work in these two intensity ranges is based primarily on aerobic processes.

The loading in the two following ranges is clearly based on a "mixed" energy metabolism with a considerable increase of the anaerobic component. The third range has high intensity loads that lead to lactate concentrations of 4 to 7 mmol/l and an increase of the oxygen consumption up to 80 to 90-95% of the maximum oxygen uptake. The fourth range enters loads within the "critical intensity" with large concentrations reaching 10 mmol/l and an oxygen consumption of 95 to 100%. The "critical intensity" signals the dividing line between mixed and anaerobic working zones.

Anaerobic loads comprise the fifth intensity range, in which lactate concentrations exceed 10 mmol/l, as well as the sixth range in which the intensity reaches maximal levels.

The values presented in this classification provide objective and directly useful information for concrete training plans in effective intensities for single parameters.

The typical content of the first intensity zone includes load ranges for the adaptation of the organism to long exertion, as well as economy and correct movement coordination. Extensive loading appears to be suitable here for young athletes (150 to 180 minutes).

The values of the second intensity range present essential information to determine intensive endurance work and to help develop specific coordination mechanisms. Loads in the range of the anaerobic threshold intensity are here favorable for the development of general (aerobic) endurance.

Our investigations indicated that children tolerate this range for a considerably long time. The loads were most effective in a 30 to 45 minutes workout. The parameter at the anaerobic threshold level can here be used as the criterion for the maximum oxygen balance (aerobic steady-state). The values should be regarded as the upper limit of the intensity of an endurance load and young athletes are advised not to exceed it.

The third intensity range consists of extensive interval runs, fartlek and longer endurance runs of 30 to 45 minutes.

The fourth intensity range covers intensive interval runs and tempo runs. Most suitable appear to be distances that correspond to 2-3 minutes in duration.

The values for the fifth and sixth intensity ranges are characteristic for the level of changes that correspond to competition-like loads and speeds.

3. STUDY RESULTS

A rational loading structure in the process of long-term, training is decisive for the achievements of an optimal capacity performance for young athletes. A narrow emphasis in training can have negative results and in the end lead to unwanted performances. These problems can be explained by two examples.

Figure 1 shows the dependence of the lactate concentration on the load intensity of a young middle distance runner in two tests. An unfavorable development in the maximal loading range is clearly noticeable, despite a certain increase of the threshold values. The result of the unfavorable training influence was only a minimal improvement in the 800m run, indicating an excessive training volume in the first intensity range. The training means failed

therefore to corresond to the demands of middle distance running.

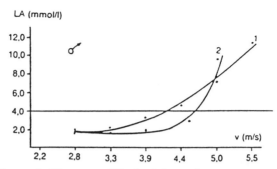

Figure 1: Changes of the lactate-performance curves of a young middle distance runner as the result of an excessive increase of the volume of training loads.

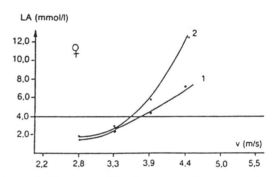

Figure 2: Changes of the lactate-performance curves of a young middle distance runner as the result of an excessive increase of the intensity of training loads.

Figure 2 shows an opposite case. The methodological fault lies in an inadequate load volume combined with excessive intensity. The expected endurance performance results were not achieved. The profile of the lactate curve is steep in the second test and the anaerobic threshold shifts to the left. In general, it can be said that in the improvement of specific performance capacity this profile flattens in young athletes, simultaneously showing a higher work intensity. This trend in elite athletes, contrary to the young runners, is clearly recognizable (Figure 3). However, considerable differences occur in the shown profiles according to event (Figure 4).

These facts indicate that an optimal balance between lactate concentration and the load intensity plays an important role in the achievements of high level performances in different endurance events. The presented examples confirm the complexity of training processes and the employment of optimal sizes and proportions of training loads. The most important role in the long-term planning of a model is in the rational distribution of the load in the single

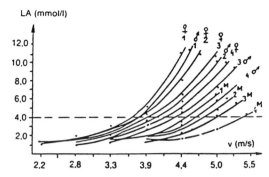

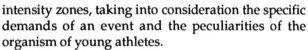

Figure 3: Changes in the lactate-performance curves according to load intensity in different level performance groups during 4 yrs of training (M=marathon; 1, 2, 3, 4,=training years).

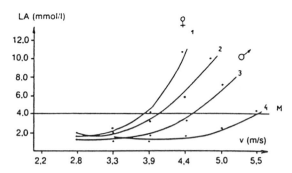

Figure 4: Comparison of lactate-performance curves in different performance groups and main distances (1=400-800 women, 2=400-800 men, 3=1500-5000 men, 4=marathon).

intensity zones, taking into consideration the specific demands of an event and the peculiarities of the organism of young athletes.

The second aspect of our investigation, based on a training analysis of top young athletes, confirmed that effectiveness of a training program is closely related to a rational structure of the training loads. It proved that the performance of young athletes depended, above all, on the total volume of the training loads. However, certain deviations

Table 1: Training load zones for young athletes in athletic endurance events.

Zone	Loading range	Loading time (min)	Lactate (mmol/l)	Heart rate (min)	Training means
Aerobic	1. Maintenance, compensation	up to 150 (180)	up to 2.0 1.5-2.5 (3.0)	130-150	Endurance runs — zone 1 Regeneration runs, Extensive runs (LA1)
	2. Development	15-45 (60)	2.5 (3.0) – 4.0	150-180	Endurance runs — zone 2 Fartlek, Cross country runs (LA 2)
Mixed	3. Intensive	8-15 (20) 1-3	4.0-7.0	170-190	Endurance runs — zone 3 Long repetition runs Extensive interval runs, Fartlek (LA 3)
	4. Critical	2-8 1-3	7.0-10.0	180-200	Tempo endurance runs, Intensive interval runs, Tempo runs, Time trials (TA)
Anaerobic	5. Over-critical	0 : 4 (2/3) 0 : 15-0 : 40	10.0	200	Speed endurance runs, Tempo runs, Time trials, (TA/SA)
	6. Maximal	up to 0 : 15	Individual		Speed development, Short repetitions at maximal and sub-maximal speeds (S)

appeared here according to specialization and training practices. There was no linear relation between the total volume and the performance in advanced junior middle distance runners (Figure 5). A negative influence on the performance can already be noted when the yearly volume exceeds 4000km. It also was discovered that certain differences occurred in the intensity zones' influence on the performance according to the demands of a specific event and the performance level of an athlete.

predominate in the woork of young athletes. A better influenced is achieved with steadily increased loads in the developmental zone (lactate 3 to 4 mmol/l). It was determined that the relationship betweeen the performance and the load volume in mixed energy zones does not follow a straight but a curved line (Figure 6). This indicates that there is a certain optimal volume of intensive training loads. Exceeding this optimal volume has a negative influence on the development of the performance.

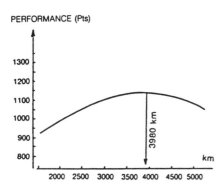

Figure 5: Dependence of the performance of young middle distance runners on the total volume of training loads.

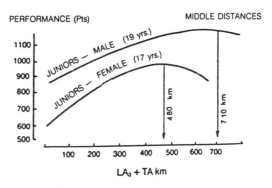

Figure 6: Dependence of the performance on the volume of training in the third and fourth intensity zone in middle distance running.

The analysis of the studies confirmed that loads in the first and the second intensity range should

4. DEVELOPMENT OF TRAINING MODELS

We attempted, based on the study results and

Table 2: A model loading structure for middle distance runners (in %)

Type of Load	Training Phases							
	Basic Training		Build-up Training			High Performance Training		
	12yrs	13yrs	14yrs	15yrs	16yrs	17yrs	18yrs	19yrs
All round development (total):	50	40	30	30	30	30	20	20
— games	35	35	35	35	35	35	35	35
— many-sided exercises	35	35	35	35	40	40	45	45
— swimming	30	30	30	30	25	25	20	20
Many-sided athletics development (total):	50	60	45	35	30	25	20	10
— sprints	30	30	40	40	45	45	50	50
— endurance runs	20	20	—	—	—	—	—	—
— jumps	25	25	35	35	35	35	30	30
— throws	25	25	25	25	20	20	20	20
Basic and specific running training (total):	Achieved within many-sided athletics develop-ment		30	35	40	45	60	70
— endurance runs LA1			92	85	78	75	67	60
LA2			5	10	15	15	20	25
LA3			—	2	2	3	4	5
— specific endurance			—	—	1	2	3	4
— rhythm and speed			2	2	3	3	3	3
— running power LK			1	1	1	2	3	2
TOTAL	100	100	100	100	100	100	100	100

Age (yrs)	LOAD VOLUME IN A YEAR (Km)							RACES (NUMBER)
	TOTAL VOLUME	LA 1	LA 2	LA 3	TA	S	LK	
13	400– 600	400– 600	–	–	–	–	–	6– 8
14	1100–1200	790– 900	160–235	–	–	40– 50	10– 15	8–10
15	1400–1600	1060–1160	235–315	30– 35	–	60– 70	15– 20	10–12
16	1800–2000	1360–1400	295–510	35– 40	20– 30	60– 70	20– 40	12–15
17	2200–2400	1520–1600	365–545	65– 75	40– 50	70– 80	40– 50	15–18
18	2400–2800	1660–1800	420–600	100–120	70– 90	75– 90	75– 90	18–20
19	2600–3000	1710–1850	500–680	130–150	100–120	80–100	80–100	

Table 3: Model parameters of training load in long-term development processes for women middle distance runner. (For abbreviations see table 1)

Age	LOAD VOLUME IN A YEAR (Km)							RACES NUMBER
	TOTAL VOLUME	LA 1	LA 2	LA 3	TA	S	LK	
13	600– 800	570– 750	–	–	–	30– 50	–	6– 8
14	1000–1200	700– 900	150– 235	–	–	40– 50	10– 15	8–10
15	1600–1800	1100–1200	275– 440	50– 70	–	60– 70	15– 20	10–12
16	2000–2200	1320–1400	500– 550	80–100	20– 40	60– 70	20– 40	12–15
17	2400–2600	1420–1450	650– 730	150–200	70– 90	70– 80	40– 50	15–18
18	2600–3000	1400–1550	700– 800	250–350	100–120	75– 90	75– 90	18–20
19	2800–3500	1450–1600	740–1000	300–500	150–200	80–100	80–100	

Table 4: Model parameters of training loads in long-term development processes for male middle distance runners. (For abbreviations see Table 1).

sport science knowledge, to develop model training loads for the single phases of training. Table 2 represents model load proportions of many-sided and specific types in the first, second and third phases in the development of middle distance runners. It provides a base for the structuring of the different intensity zones that vary according to the energy availability (aerobic, aerobic-anaerobic and anaerobic). The aim is to determine the optimal load ranges in the single intensity zones.

The model parameters, determined after many years of observation of male and female middle distance runners, are presented in Tables 3 and 4.

The models determine the direction of the training influence and allow the evaluation of how well the tasks have been achieved, as far as the effect of training is concerned. It appears that the general principles of long-term development of a specific event have been taken into consideration.

Training means (in km)	Girls			Boys		
	Training Year					
	1	2	3	1	2	3
LA 1	440	720	1260	600	850	1325
LA 2	120	220	378	150	274	480
LA 3	–	–	50	–	–	70
Others	32	48	94	40	60	100
Races (number)	8	12	18	10	16	25
Total volume (km)	600	1000	1800	800	1200	2000

Table 5: The structure of the endurance loads in the phase of the general many-sided preparation.

Consequently aerobic loads dominate the model for young runners. This provides a base for the following intensive and narrower approach to a specific distance.

The share of the loads in higher intensity ranges, with mixed and anaerobic energy consumption increases in the following training phases. It appears that the proposed criteria helps to make the training and development of young distance runners more effective and at the same time prevents the exploitation of the developing organism. The usefulness of the determined training loads are confirmed in the collected data in Tables 5 and 6.

Training periods	Volume of running loads in different intensity zones (km)					
	LA 1	LA 2	LA 3	TA	S	Total
Preparation period	1170	690	250	70	20	2200
Competition period	750	300	180	135	35	1400
Transition period	110	—	—	—	—	110
Total volume	2030	990	430	205	55	3700

Table 6:The structure of the running loads in a yearly training cycle of an advanced junior middle distance runner. (Holder of Poland's 800m and 1500m junior records).

A LONG-TERM DEVELOPMENT PLAN FOR MIDDLE DISTANCE RUNNERS

by M. Linets, USSR

A structure of interrelated stages of a long term development plan for middle distance runners in which various stages of the structure are determined by statistically proven age ranges for the optimal performance.

The contemporary literature regards training as a multi-year process that consists of a series of interrelated stages without sharp boundaries. These stages follow from one into the other according to the adaptation of the body to systematic training effects. Nevertheless, it is possible to determine the approximate age and duration limits for the separate stages of training, based on the optimal age of best performances in a multi-year plan.

SPECIALIZED TRAINING

An analysis of the best middle distance runners in the world indicates that top results are usually achieved after 8 to 12 years of specialized training at an age range of 23 to 27 years. The first major successes are reached at 20 to 22 and high level results are maintained up to about 32 years of age. Based on this information it appears that an optimal age to begin specialized training in middle distance running would be at 14 to 15. This would allow the required 8 to 12 years of specific training to reach best results during the optimal 23 to 27 years age range.

However, practical experience and studies have shown that preliminary all-round preparations over a period of two to three years must precede specialization. This period is required to establish a base of all-round physical performance capacities, as well as to allow an evaluation of the young athlete's potential for middle distance running. Consequently the first stage of preliminary training should begin between 12 to 13 years and is concluded between 14 to 15 years. An even earlier start of the preliminary training stage is desirable, provided it does not lead to an earlier specialization. It should be kept in mind that specific training must be started at an optimal age and the training program planned to reach best performances during the correct high performance age.

There is a sharp improvement of results in middle distance running during the first five to six years of specialized training. Research has shown that the basic factors which determine the improvement and create favorable conditions for success in the following years is an increase of the training volume and load. This continues until further increases in the training volume are not accompanied by a corresponding improvement in performance.

NARROW SPECIALIZATION

Once this situation occurs, the first specialization stage has been completed and there is a need to start training according to a narrower specific approach. The narrow specialized methods should lead to further substantial improvement through new stresses applied to the training processes without significant changes to the total volume.

It is common to find that talented middle distance runners achieve their first notable successes during the first three or four years of training mainly through an increased training load. However, attempts to force further the volume or intensity in specialized training, as a rule, do not bring the desired results. They can frequently lead to adaptational disturbances in the organism and, thus, overtraining. They can be avoided by significant changes in the training volume and intensity with emphasis given primarily to the development of the individual capacities of the runner.

Further improvements can be achieved by employing specific micro-and macrocycles to develop a more economical running technique, to improving tactics and to exploiting more efficiently the training level achieved at this stage. Provided the previous training stages have been correctly planned and executed, talented runners will now begin the stage of a maximum realization of their individual performance capacities. This allows for a further improvement of results over the following four or five years.

It is unlikely that additional improvement will take place after the maximum realization stage at the end of 11 to 12 years of specialized training. During this phase of a runner's career a new long term training plan has to be designed to maintain the performance level as much as possible. New training methods and means, including some non-traditional, have to be employed with variable training loads and intensities in order for many runners to continue competing at a high level for another four to six years.

Training must not be stopped suddenly when the competitive career of a runner comes to an end. Forced decreases as well as increases in training loads bring about not only functional but also pathological changes in the body. It is therefore necessary to change gradually from specialized to general training. The multi-year development plan does consequently include also a gradual tapering off stage.

SUMMARY

In summary it can be said that it is possible to formulate a methodological structure of a multi-year training plan for middle distance runners, based on the following principles:

- The first preliminary all-round preparation stage of middle distance runners should begin not later than 12 to 13 years of age
- The specialized training phase should begin in the period ranging from 14-15 to 17-18 years of age
- The maximum realization stage should be planned to start in the 18-19 to 21-22 age range. It is the stage of maximal realization of the individual capacities of a runner that will coincide with the optimal (23 to 27 years) age for the best performance
- A maintenance stage should begin after 11 to 12 years of specialized training, as further performance improvements are now unlikely.

THE TRAINING OF YOUNG DISTANCE RUNNERS— INTRODUCING THE THEORIES OF OLAV KARIKOSK

by Ari Paunonen, Finland

A critical summary of the views and theories on the development of young distance runners by well-known Estonian coach Olav Karikosk, stressing the need to avoid early specialization.

The results of Karikosk's studies show clearly the correct type of training methods for young distance runners that are most likely to produce the best and most consistent performances at adult age. His findings make questionable the values of the training systems "developed" by many well-known distance running coaches.

There is every reason to ask what will happen to the training of young distance runners in the future. Are we going to repeat the mistakes of the past by stressing anaerobic training? The same question is applicable to the racing program of youngsters, critically observed by Karikosk during his short visit to Finland.

There appears to be little doubt that Karikosk's conclusions on how to approach the training of young middle distance runners deserve attention. The conclusions have been derived from years of practical experience and gathering of data on the development and training of a large number of the world's best middle distance exponents.

One of the interesting findings revealed in Karikosk's studies, is the fact that as many as 63% of the international level of distance runners have been involved in soccer. He believes that soccer is an excellent game for the development of running capacities because it demands many different varieties of natural and unforced running. However, soccer develops running only in a free and unorganized concept of a game so often played by young boys. This, in the opinion of the Estonian coach, is very different from the contemporary approach to organized soccer training that fails to meet the basic nature of running.

Whether it is soccer, which dominates the sporting scene in Central Europe and England, or cross country skiing which is so popular among the children in Finland, the results of Karikosk's studies should be seriously looked at by all authorities in charge of children's sport. Based on this theory it appears to be obvious that distance running performances can in the future be improved by adopting a less strenuous approach to training. It should not follow the familiar demanding structure that can be replaced by a free, less frightening, natural development.

Karikosk became seriously interested in the training of young distance runners while teaching physical education in a large technical school. After four years of teaching he discovered that the group of selected young athletes he was coaching progressed relatively slower than students who approached sporting activities less seriously and often missed training sessions.

It became obvious to Karikosk that the training methods he had applied were wrong. This inspired him to find better and more successful training methods for the development of young distance runners, an aim that has strongly influenced his work over several decades. It began with experiments involving a large number of students and was followed up by collecting information on the development and training of the leading distance runners from all corners of the world.

EXPERIMENTAL METHODS

In his training experiments Karikosk employed the following activities in the training programs of young distance runners:

1. *Many-sided physical preparation*
    *   School physical education periods
    *   Indoor gymnastics training
    *   Learning the techniques of several track and field events.

2. *Sprint training*
   - Accelerations over 80 to 100m
   - Starting practice over 20 to 40m from standing and crouch positions with full recoveries
   - The development of maximal speed over 20 to 60m distances from a flying start with full recoveries.

3. *General endurance training*
   - Aerobic running with a heart rate around 120 to 150 beats a minute
   - General endurance development activities, such as soccer, cross country skiing, swimming, basketball, etc.

4. *Specific endurance training*
   - Repetition and interval runs over 800 to 1000m with a heart rate about 150 to 170 beats a minute
   - Repetition and interval runs over 200 to 400m with a heart rate exceeding 170 beats a minute.

The athletes involved in the experiment were divided into three groups. All groups used the above outlined program in their training. The only difference that took place was the age the youngsters began specific endurance training. Group A started specific endurance training at the age of 15 years, Group B applied this method at the age of 17 years and Group C two years later at the age of 19 years.

The number of competitions was also strictly determined. It was limited to 10 races a year in the 15 to 16 years age range. The 17 to 18 years age group participated in no more than 15 races.

At the start of the experiments the young athletes in Group A had a average best 800m time of 2:30.3 minutes, Group B had a 2:27.8 minute best average and Group C 2:28.1 minutes. Without going into the details of how these young athletes progressed and their rate of improvement, the Group C performers showed a clear advantage over the other two groups as adults. These were the athletes who began specific endurance training at the age of 19 years.

Four athletes from Group C represented Estonia and the Soviet Union as adult competitors. In contrast, Group B produced only one national representative and not a single athlete from Group A reached this performance level.

INTERNATIONAL SURVEY

Additional studies by Karikosk, based on a large number of individual questionnaires and information available from literature, confirmed his theory. This extended study, conducted during the years Karikosk was working on his Masters Degree at the University of Tartu, Estonia, included information on 667 successful middle and long distance runners (Olympic medalists, world record and world class performers).

An analysis of their performances, based on the age the athletes began specific endurance training, clearly showed the same pattern discovered by Karikosk in his earlier experiments. Tables 1 and 2 represent summaries of this analysis, using the above-mentioned age limit of specific endurance training for classification.

Table 1: A comparison of the success rate of Estonian, USSR and world distance runners according to the age they began specific endurance training.

METHOD	ESTONIAN	USSR	WORLD
800 METERS			
A	2	1	26
B	5	4	39
C	13	21	119
1500 METERS			
A	0	2	25
B	8	2	30
C	12	19	117

Table 2: A survey of middle and long distance runners who reached international level performances according to the age they began specific endurance training.

METHOD	INTERNATIONAL LEVEL	OLYMPIC WINNERS WORLD RECORDS
A	59	5
B	129	18
C	473	71

NOTE: Specific endurance training began:
A—15 years; B—17 years; C—19 years.

Both tables leave no doubt that young athletes, who delayed the start of specific endurance training (in this survey until 19 years), have been by far the most successful. The figures provide ample evidence for coaches of young distance runners to take a serious look at the training methods they are currently employing.

CONCLUSIONS

Karikosk sums up his conclusions in seven major points:

1. It would be wrong to state that the use of

specific endurance training is completely unacceptable at the age of 15 to 16 years. However, this method is extremely dangerous because of the difficulties in determining individually suitable training loads and intensities.

2. Extensive specific endurance training in the 14 to 17 years age range makes large energy demands at the developmental stage of the organism.

3. It appears that an efficient and by far a safer method for young distance runners is an approach that concentrates on the many-sided development of aerobic endurance and speed.

4. Outstanding performances by young athletes in middle and long distance running are by no means an indication of top-class results at adult age.

5. Most athletes who have reached world class performances in distance events have during their growth years participated in sprinting activities that are particularly suitable for the development of the cardiovascular system.

6. There are some exceptions among the early developers, capable of tolerating oxygen debt better than their counterparts. Typical examples are such athletes as Cruz, Ryun and Cram.

7. Most of the top-class distance runners in the 14 to 17 years age range have participated extensively in a variety of sporting activities (soccer, cross country skiing, basketball, swimming, rugby, handball, orienteering, etc.).

DOUBLE PERIODIZATION FOR SCHOOL MIDDLE DISTANCE RUNNERS

by Les Roberts, Canada

A detailed developmental plan, based on a six-phase double periodized training year, for high school middle distance runners.

Middle distance running in high schools should be an arena for developing future international runners. However, this can only be true if more young athletes are directed into developmental programs, rather than the multi-season racing schedules available to them. It has been known for young athletes to try for peak performances in fall cross country championships, indoor championships, outdoor high school spring championships and summer age class championships in consecutive seasons, and consecutive years. It is easy to see that if these young runners are encouraged to participate in this championship circus, there can be little real development going on. So then, what form should this development take? The answer to this question is, of course, dependent on the characteristics of the individual athlete, but standard sports training theory can give a general approach.

Standard sports training theory indicates that the training year, and the training life time, is a series of phases of different intensity loadings. That is, training is *not* a continuously upward spiral. What is optimum for one level of performance is not optimal for another, higher level. There is also the summation effect of training loads. That is, training loads that can lead to a peak performance at one level, if continued for too long, will lead to overtraining. Therefore, a particular level of performance cannot be kept up. Indeed, this peak level of competitive readiness will impede the acquisition of a new higher level of performance. Once a particular level of performance is reached, it must be brought down to a lower level by greatly reducing the intensity of training, before the rebuilding process to a new, higher level can commence. The planning of this cyclic nature of training is called periodization. Periodization separates training activities into general preparatory training, event special training and competition

specific training to describe the workout emphasis in the different phases of the year. The actual training activities in each of these areas would be different for each individual athlete and each event type. For high school middle distance runners, however, the following concepts correspond to these general areas:

General Preparatory Training—agility work, flexibility work, aerobic power runs, restorative running, stair and hill running, maximum strength, aerobic capacity runs or intervals, rest, other sports, games, skipping, cycling, skiing, etc.

Event Special Training—progressive intervals, tempo workouts, elastic strength, technique drills, aerobic efficiency runs or intervals, lactate (anaerobic capacity) workouts, leg speed workouts, fartlek, stress workouts, anaerobic efficiency workouts, stair and hill bounding, etc.

Competition Specific Training—pace intervals, pure speed, repetition workouts, test runs, strength endurance, surge runs, alternate runs, speed endurance, anaerobic power workouts, time trials, etc.

Periodization also takes into account at what specific time of the year the athletes wish to achieve a maximum competition climax or peak. This would be different for different events, the length of the competitive season, and whether or not the athlete is to compete in major games or championships with separate associated qualifying trials. Therefore, careful planning is needed to prepare the athlete for the achievement of an optimal improvement in performance and for a definite peak to the competitive season. The ability to peak at a prescribed time is the essence of periodization; without it, training can be wasted. The main types of organization that are used are single and double periodization.

In general, single periodization in the training year is divided into six (6) phases. Phase 1 is "training to be able to train later." Phases 2 and 4 are planned using preparation objectives, while phases 3 and 5 pursue competitive advantage. Phase 6 is a rehabilitation phase. Some details of the individual characteristics of these phases follow:

Phase 1—this is the longest phase in the annual cycle and should take up 1/3 of the year or about four months. The aim of this phase is to lay a base for training during the rest of the year through the use of mostly general preparatory training. A suggested ratio of training in this phase for high school middle distance runners would be 60% general preparatory training, 25% event special training and 15% competition specific training, counting all training units used. This necessitates a high volume of work and a gradual increase of intensity throughout the phase, so that the runner will be able to accept the high intensity of work of phase 2.

Phase 2—this phase lasts about two months and is the hardest working phase of the year. The running volume is decreased slightly and the intensity is increased progressively through event special training, up to and slightly beyond the levels anticipated for performances in phase 3. A suggested ratio for this phase is 30% general preparatory training, 45% event special training and 25% competition specific training.

Phase 3—the task of this phase is to stabilize training so that a high level of competitive performance can be obtained. Therefore, overall intensity is slightly decreased, while competition-specific training is increased. A suggested ratio for the training units in this phase is 25% general preparatory training, 30% event special training and 45% competition specific training. Phase 3 lasts 6-9 weeks and by 3-5 weeks from the start of this phase, athletes should expect to be within 2.5% of their previous best performance.

Phase 4—this phase returns to a more basic training to allow the athlete a respite from the competitions of phase 3 and to gear up to the peak performances of phase 5. Therefore, competition-specific training is reduced, competitions are eliminated, and general event special training is increased. A ratio of training loads for this phase would be 40% general preparatory training, 40% event special training, and 20% competition specific training. This phase can last 3-6 weeks depending on the extent of phases 3 and 5.

Phase 5—the athlete should be able to reach peak performances after three or four competitions. The emphasis is on the maintenance of the training effects achieved, while concentration is on sharpening and receiving adequate rest. Therefore, overall intensity is at about 80% to 95% of that of level 2 and competition special work is at its highest. A suggested ratio for this phase is 20% general preparatory training, 25% event special training, and 55% competition specific training.

Phase 6—after the peak competition the athlete needs to recover from the stresses and strains put on the system. A transition period of active rest is needed before training can start again. A training ratio for this phase would be 75% general preparatory training, 20% event special training, and 5% competition-specific training. Three to six weeks of low key activity will bring down the competitive readiness and recharge the batteries for a higher development in the next season.

Normal double periodization uses these same six phases, but repeats phases 1, 2 and 3 before going on to phases 4, 5 and 6. The form of double periodization that I recommend for high school middle distance runners uses the addition of a second active rest (phase 6) phase following cross country to ensure recovery from this racing season. By having strong competitive periods only in fall cross country and spring track seasons, and the fact that the aerobic stresses of cross country do not tear down the body as acutely as those of middle distance track running, this form of double periodization can be used effectively to enhance the development of high school runners. Further, by dividing the second phase 3 into two shorter, easier parts (phases 3b and 3c) and separating these parts by phase 4 and low-key indoor competitions can be used to advantage. In this way the young athlete can compete in all seasons, except the summer age class competitions, without jeopardizing future development.

This ability to compete in all seasons keeps the young athlete well motivated, as long as the athlete understands *not* to expect peak performances all year long. Even summer age class races can be used to keep motivation high if the athlete does *not* change the training away from that which is appropriate for the training phase going through that time (i.e., do inappropriate high intensity, peak training workouts at the wrong time). The makeup of the yearly training plan following this scheme would look like the following:

Phase 1a—July and August (8 weeks long)

The objective is to gradually increase the weekly mileage up to as much as 10% more than last year's maximum. One training session alternates between aerobic capacity intervals and aerobic efficiency intervals. Another training session alternates between a short sustained run and a very long easy run. The other sessions can be steady or easy runs with some strides afterward.

Phase 2a—August and September (5 weeks long)

The objective is to gradually increase the amount of event special cross country work and increase the speed of all runs. The mileage is about 80% of that of phase 1a and long progressive interval training is given emphasis.

Phase 3a—Sept., Oct. and Nov. (5 to 6 weeks long)

The objective is to race well in cross country runs. The mileage is about 60% of that of phase 1a and competition specific cross country workouts are added.

Phase 6a—November (3 weeks long)

The objective is to have an active rest to rejuvenate the body's systems. Other sports, games, and any activity that is not normally considered a training activity are engaged in at a low intensity level.

Phase 1b—December and January (8 weeks long)

The objectives and training activities are similar to those of phase 1a. The mileage can be further increased up to as much as 15% more than that of phase 1a.

Phase 2b—January and February (2 to 3 weeks long)

The objectives are the same as phase 2a, but event special work is designed for track racing instead of cross country. The mileage is 80% of that of phase 1b and progressive interval workouts are increased.

Phase 3b—February and March (3 to 5 weeks long)

The objective is to use time trials or indoor races to pinpoint strengths and weaknesses. Track competition specific workouts are given emphasis and the mileage is cut to about 60% of that of phase 1b.

Phase 4—March and April (3 to 4 weeks long)

The objective is to lower the intensity of workouts so that the body can recover from the stresses of phase 3b. The mileage is increased to about 70% of that of phase 1b, competition-specific workouts are reduced, and aerobic intervals are returned.

Phase 3c—April and early May (4 to 5 weeks long)

The objective is to continue phase 3b using workouts geared to the strengths and weaknesses found before. Progressive interval and competition-specific training are the key here. Mileage is again cut to about 60% of that of phase 1b.

Phase 5—May and early June (3 to 4 weeks long)

The objective is to reach a peak performance. The mileage is cut to about 50% of that of phase 1b in order to concentrate on speed and pace activities. The intensity of training is a little lower than that of phase 3c because of the high level of competitions. Training centers around the competition-specific but all systems must be used through appropriate maintenance workouts.

Phase 6b—June (3 weeks long)

The objective here is to have a complete or active rest to rebuild the body's resources for the next year. Use the same activities as those of phase 6a, only at a lower intensity level yet.

It is to be understood that the above plan is a compromise to allow for the available high school programs, as it is best to keep even aspiring international runners with their peer groups as much as possible.

It should be noted, however, that double periodization is not recommended for very young athletes and long distance runners. The extra stresses of standard double periodization can be detrimental to very young and growing athletes and does not provide a strong enough base for superior middle distance performances. Therefore, I would suggest that the first two years of high school running be used to gradually adapt the athletes to the above plan by using a less stressful approach.

Attention should also be given to the individual training units and microcycles that make up each phase. Each phase uses these shorter microcycles so that concentration on one particular training objective can be emphasized and to help prevent stagnation of performance. Microcycles consist of a number of individual units in some ratio of training units to rest or easy units. For many younger runners the ratio of 6:1 (training to rest) can lose its value and a regular cycle of 3:1 may suit this athlete's development better. Poorly organized training units may bring objectives into conflict; e.g., when speed and endurance units are too close together, maximal development of either is impossible. Similarly, when repetitions and sets are rushed, development can be impaired. However, the above double periodization plan, as a place to start programming, will help to reduce the over-stressing of high school athletes. Following a plan like the one above will also help these athletes adjust to any university athletic program they may encounter in their future.

In Ontario universities the middle distance runner is usually a mature athlete with some years of background training. Therefore, there are fewer restrictions inhibiting athletic development than for the high school athlete. The absence of a spring championship season makes the year very much easier to program, but in general the same considerations and concepts used to program high school schedules are applicable to university syllabuses as well.

For Ontario universities, however, academics are usually of paramount importance! The fact that there is a heavy academic and exam period every November/December and March/April cannot be overlooked. This presents little problem for athletes who wish to peak for the fall, cross country or summer outdoor season. But, as the the major university track season is during the indoor months of February and March, university athletes, who wish to peak for this indoor season, will have difficulty arranging the 3b phase, as suggested in November and December. Therefore, for some athletes this 3b phase may have to be eliminated or at least more extensive use of time trials be made.

The Ontario Universities' fall track season can be used to good advantage by all athletes, as some competition-specific work needs to be done in all phases. The university athlete then, may use one of three main types of periodization competition program: a schedule for a major peak in the fall or cross country season with a second peak during the indoor season; a schedule for a major peak in the indoor season with a second peak during the summer; or a schedule to peak in the summer with a minor peak during the indoor season (this scheme allows the athlete to compete well in major national or international games).

REFERENCES

Dick, F.W. (1980). *Sports Training Principles*. Lepus, London.
Matveyev, L.P. (1981). *Fundamentals of Sports Training*. Moscow.

DEVELOPMENT OF YOUNG MIDDLE DISTANCE RUNNERS

by Klaus Roth, Australia

A summary of the problem areas in the development of young middle distance runners, looking at long-term many-sided training, the physiological factors and the psychological problems.

There appears to be a need for an appraisal of the under-age competition structure to fit it into a desirable and generally recommended development plan for young athletes. A closer look into this problem reveals three areas which are of particular concern and are discussed in this text.

LONG-TERM ALL-ROUND DEVELOPMENT

This refers particularly to the development of elite distance runners, but is also applicable to the all-round personal development of each individual.

The almost unanimous opinion of leading coaches is that an athlete's physical development requires a many-sided, non-specific, long-term approach during the childhood and teenage years, with specialization only occurring in the late teens. Arens (1) canvassed these opinions thoroughly and summed them up as follows:

- GDR coaches Scholich, Loffler and Hendel say that early specialization brings success but means long-term lack of progress
- West German coach Weissenborn claims that an athlete has about 5-8 years to reach his ultimate performance. Therefore the later the specialization, the greater the chance for the athlete to reach his full potential
- U.S.S.R. coach Karikosk states that specific running training is only successful if built on a wide base of all-round development in the years of growth. He found in a study of international athletes that the overwhelming majority of world-class performers and Olympic winners in distance running did not commence specialized training until their late teens. Karikosk concludes that "specialization is frequently occurring at a far too early age" and "biased training loads, either aerobic or anaerobic, for

the young developing athlete must be prevented."

PHYSIOLOGICAL PROBLEMS

There has at times been unnecessarily extreme concern expressed about training for the various athletic events, especially endurance running, and the possible short- and long-term detrimental physical effect on the child's body.

However, the Australian Sports Medicine Federation's position paper on Children in Sport (2) states that "there is no evidence that children are at any greater risk of injury than adults when training at a quality and quantity relative to their respective capacity," although it states that children are more susceptible to body heat fluctuations and care needs to be taken with "at risk" groups.

The paper comes to the conclusion that endurance training and competition should be encouraged, provided that training is carefully programmed and the child maintains enthusiasm and enjoyment of the activity, and that an all-round development program is not precluded. Consequently the main concern appears to be in the finding of correct competitive distances for young distance runners and in the dangers of an early specialization.

Dr. McNee, for example, found problems of acute distress among the competitors in the 1985 Queensland schools cross-country championships. He blamed the unsuitably long distances and the pressure on the children by their parents and teachers for this.

The warning against specialized training during puberty has been published by several overseas authorities. They maintain that growth during puberty means that specialization at this age may not provide sufficient recovery and will restrict the required all-round development of the young athlete.

In summary, it appears that there is unlikely to be any need for concern for the physical well-being of the young athletes, provided care is taken in the programming of the training and competitions in the young age range.

PSYCHOLOGICAL PROBLEMS

Psychological factors in competition and training, including their relationship with the athlete's total environment, are considered to be an important factor in the development of the young athlete. Yet, it appears that very few practical efforts have been made to overcome these problems, particularly as they relate to junior competition.

"Burning out" is a term frequently used when top athletes fail to go on with sport, or drop out altogether. Flippin (4) evaluates the high stress training and competition on the American high school circuit and the physical and emotional effect of this on many young athletes. He quotes Cerutty, who states that the elite athletes, who are mentally "tough," are the ones to succeed and there is a mutually dependent relationship between doing well and tough-mindedness. When things don't go well it is not as easy to be "tough" and consequently only the fittest survive.

The same principle applies, perhaps more so, to the less able athletes of all ages. Wheeler (5) states that competition introduced at too early an age, with the resultant tension and strain brought on by pressure to win, may cause a sense of failure in young children, so that interest in the sport and a desire to participate later in life can be lost.

Both Sandstrom (6) and Martens (7) evaluate the age group competitive environment, where attitudes towards athletics are formed early, and where children are disillusioned with initial lack of success, perhaps partially due to different maturation rates. Martens also mentions the danger of the successful early maturer who finds it hard to adjust when the other athletes catch up.

This area has also been one of Clohessy's (3) major concerns and his articles strongly show that "it is interest which captivates the young, not pressure which erodes potential." Wardlaw (8) concurs with Clohessy in the need to set achievable goals and the need to look at "winning" as the by-product of doing something well, instead of being "first."

Otherwise interest will be lost because of continual failure.

From a more general point of view, the psychological stress factors of children in sport has been a major topic of discussion for some time, particularly among physical educators. Connors and Clarke (9), for example, state that "premature involvement in major games, over-exuberant parents and the early stress on the status of a winner, can make a child feel totally inadequate."

Tutko (10) states that "kids want to participate as much as possible in an activity and winning only becomes very important in the mid-teens."

Robertson (11) in a survey of grade 7 children in Australia found that the most significant turn-on in involvement in sport was the intrinsic rewards, i.e., involvement for its own sake, and that dropouts occurred largely due to factors in sports programs, i.e., boring, no fun, etc. He also states that sports organizations have a challenge to present more attractive programs.

While the previous references obviously point out the dangers of a stressful and unenjoyable competitive environment, nowhere have the problems of young athletes been better expressed than in the article "Growing with Running" (12) by an author unknown, who makes the following statements:

- "Youth is still a time of playing, growing, exploring
- Young athletes are a bundle of contradictions
- They're more flexible than mature ones in certain circumstances, and more fragile in others
- They take their setbacks harder, but they are quicker to bounce back from them
- They have fewer inhibitions, but the ones they have can seem gigantic
- Their craving for recognition reaches a peak in their teens, but they often react clumsily to attention
- They want independence and yet need more support than older runners
- At no time in life is one so capable of fanatical attachment to an activity, and at no other time can this turn so quickly to indifference as interests change."

REFERENCES

1. Arens, O. "Train or Play for Young Runners." ATFCA Level III accreditation thesis.
2. Australian Sports Medicine Federation. "Position Statement: Children in Sport-Endurance Running." *Sports Health*, Vol. 2, No. 2, 1984.
3. Flippin, R. "Burning Out." *The Runner*, July 1981.
4. Wheeler, H.G. "Athletic Events for Lower Ages Ranges." *S.A. Physical Education Bulletin* 1972.
5. Sandstrom, E.R. "Training and Competition of Young Athletes," *Modern Athlete and Coach*, Vol. 13, No. 4, 1973.

6. Martens, R. "Biological Time Clocks Differ." *Modern Athlete and Coach*, Vol. 18, No. 4, 1980.
7. Clohessy, P. "The Benefits of Distance Running to Young Athletes." *Sports Coach*, Vol. 8, No. 4, 1983.
8. Wardlaw, C. "Choice of Sacrifice." *Australian Runner*, April 1985.
9. Connors, T. and Clarke, L. "Dear Teacher." *Northern Territory Physical Education Branch*, 1981.
10. Tutko, R. "A Question of Balance." *Sports Fitness*, June 1985.
11. Robertson, I. "Sport in the View of South Australian Children." *Sports Coach*, March 1984.
12. Author unknown. "Growing with Running." *The Young Runner*, World Publications, 1973.

Gun lap in the 1984 NCAA 1500 final, won by Claudette Groenendaal of Oregon (#213).